SCHOOLBOY,
SERVANT,
GWR APPRENTICE

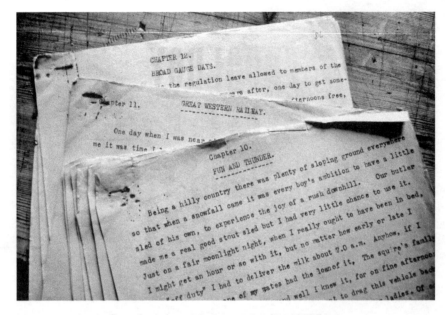

Pages from the original typescript. (David Wilkins)

Schoolboy, Servant, GWR Apprentice

The Memoirs of Alfred Plumley
1880–1892

Edited by
David Wilkins

Cover illustrations

Front, clockwise from top: Mendip Lodge (Stan Croker Collection (original photograph *c.*1935 by George Love Dafnis)); The Cornishman Express passing the signal cabin at Worle Junction (Rev. A.H. Malan / Great Western Trust). *Back, from top*: A handwritten page from the original manuscript (David Wilkins); GWR locomotive *Leopard* (Great Western Trust).

First published 2017

The History Press
The Mill, Brimscombe Port
Stroud, Gloucestershire, GL5 2QG
www.thehistorypress.co.uk

British Library Cataloguing in Publication Data.
A catalogue record for this book is available from the British Library.

ISBN 978 0 7509 6993 2

Typesetting and origination by The History Press
Printed and bound by CPI Group (UK) Ltd

CONTENTS

Acknowledgements

I am grateful to the following organisations and individuals for their help with my research: Jane Dixon and John Gowar of the Langford History Group; Raye Green and David Hart of Worle History Society; Elaine Arthurs at STEAM: Museum of the Great Western Railway, Swindon; Laurence Waters at the Great Western Trust Museum and Archive, Didcot; Sir David and Lady Wills, who allowed me to visit the gardens at Langford Court; Stan and Gill Croker; Charlie Wilkins.

I also thank the following people who read and commented on various sections of the draft book for me: Sue Forber; Mandy Hoang; Paul Morris; Anthony Orchard; Amy Rigg; John Sadden; Laurence Waters.

Every effort has been made to trace all copyright holders and to obtain their permission for the use of copyright material. To rectify any omissions, please contact the author care of the publisher so that we can incorporate such corrections in future reprints or editions.

INTRODUCTION

On a cold, thoroughly miserable afternoon in January 2014, still in my scarf and woolly hat, zipped up in my warm coat, I was rooting around in the lots for sale at an auction saleroom in a Dorset seaside town. The wind off Lyme Bay rattled the windows. It felt colder indoors than outdoors.

In auction salerooms you'll often hear people say, 'If only it could talk', in reference to some ancient, rustic chair or a pretty brooch that may have been a lover's gift. Occasionally, a little bit of research can reveal the past lives of such objects but, for the most part, furniture and jewellery, like china, bronze and glass, tend to be rather aloof. They regard their past as a private matter. It is in the dark spaces beneath the tables, where the battered cardboard boxes are, that there is gossip to be heard. Here are the lower social classes of the saleroom – the 'mixed lots', the 'miscellaneous items' and the 'ephemera'. Here are bundles of letters tied up with string, old notebooks and diaries, and dog-eared documents that were once of the very greatest importance. These things are really nothing *but* a story.

After about half an hour, just when I was beginning to wish I had stayed home where it was warm, I picked up from such a box an old folder, clearly some decades old. It contained maybe 100 typewritten sheets held together in small batches by rusted staples. The paper was rather tatty and discoloured and the uneven lines suggested that the typewriter's best days were already behind it when the typescript was made, but the top sheet of the bundle carried an intriguing title, though one which gave little away: *Chip of the*

Mendips. As my cold, numbed fingers turned the pages, the document was revealed to be a memoir of some kind, written by an elderly man recalling his rural childhood and adolescence. It looked interesting. By the end of the sale the next day, it belonged to me.

That evening I sat down to read the memoir; the bare bones of it are easily summarised. It was written anonymously and described the life of a boy growing up in a village in the Mendip Hills in Somerset in the late nineteenth century. It began with the writer's first day of school at the age of 5. Just after his twelfth birthday, his schooldays came to end and he immediately went into service as a pageboy at the 'big house' nearby. At 16, with the help of the kindly lady of the house who wanted to encourage him into a trade, he took up a station staff apprenticeship with the Great Western Railway (GWR). Initially he worked as a 'lad porter' at a village station and later he was transferred to the 'great city' of Bristol to gain more experience.

When the writer turned 18 in 1892, his job with the GWR was confirmed as permanent. On that same day, to his great relief, he was transferred from Bristol back to a country station, at which point the memoir ended. However, the memoirist assured the reader that he went on to become a successful railwayman – his entire working life was to be spent with the GWR.

The typescript itself was undated, but piecing together the clues it was possible to work out that the memoir was written sometime between 1954 and 1956, when the author was in his early 80s. He wrote it by hand in a notebook and it was typed up by a friend or relative; one leaf of the original handwritten version had survived and was loose inside the folder.

Of course, the immediate challenge was to identify the memoirist, but that presented a puzzle. The writer names himself just twice in the 40,000 words of text, on both occasions reporting other people speaking to him or about him. The first time he refers to himself only by the forename 'Alfred'; the second time – in reference to his surname – only by the initial 'P'. The places where he lived, went to school and worked are all given fictitious names (this little deceit, incidentally, dawning on me only after a frustrating hour poring over increasingly large-scale maps, first of the Mendip Hills and then of the whole of Somerset).

Because the place names were invented, there was of course the possibility that 'Alfred' and/or the surname 'P' were also fabrications. It could easily have been that the memoirist would prove impossible ever to identify, in which case this book could not have been written. On page eighty-four of the typescript, however, there was a crucial number: 15718. This number was the secret code in this spy story, the co-ordinates on the pirate's treasure map, the combination to the safe holding the stolen documents. It was the writer's GWR staff number, the number that appeared on his wage slip every week for forty-five years, the number that might give him a name.

The staff records of the GWR going back to the middle of the nineteenth century are stored at The National Archives in Kew and can be searched online. The records are not filed sequentially by staff number, so the only way to find our man was to look up – with fingers crossed that Alfred was his real name – every individual 'Alfred' who started work with the GWR in the later 1880s or early 1890s (it was possible to roughly estimate this time period from other information in the memoir). After I had ploughed through the first four- or five-dozen ghosts of Victorian engine drivers, signalmen, porters, booking clerks, fitters and coachbuilders named Alfred, the number in the right-hand column of the staff records suddenly matched the number in the notebook on my desk. There, blinking in the spotlight after more than a century shut flat in the GWR staff ledger, was the author of the memoir: Alfred James Plumley.

A quick cross reference to the 1881 census records soon found the very same Alfred James Plumley, then a 'scholar' aged 6, the son of a coachman, living in Lower Langford, a village – as expected – in the Mendip region of Somerset. Our story had a beginning.

This book then takes a stroll through Alfred's life from the day he started school in 1879 to the day in 1892 when he became officially and permanently, in his own words, 'a uniformed servant of the mighty GWR'.

For someone whose schooling was, by his own account, no more than rudimentary, Alfred's memoir is extremely well written. His prose style is certainly simple – at times almost conversational – but always expressive and engaging. He describes village life vividly and the Mendip landscape with great affection. His memories are full of human interest and, 130 years on, the historical detail is fascinating.

Alfred's approach to telling his story was to string together those experiences and incidents from his childhood and adolescence that were still memorable to him sixty years later. In other words, the memoir is essentially a series of short tales or anecdotes that had lived on in Alfred's mind – as, indeed, similar experiences stay sharply focused in all our minds. On a superficial level these experiences are 'ordinary', that is to say childhood and adolescence were for Alfred much the same as they are for most of the rest of us. Some good things happened to him, some funny things happened, some sad things happened; however, it is this very ordinariness that makes the memoir compelling. Somehow, in the simplicity of his storytelling, Alfred manages to touch the universal nature of these types of experience and their place in individual memory. Despite the huge cultural and material differences between then and now, it is remarkable how familiar Alfred's experiences seem. But then, one's first day at school is one's first day at school, whether it happened thirty years ago or 130 years ago. Family life is family life and friends are friends. Having a laugh with your workmates is no different in the twenty-first century from how it was in the nineteenth. That dreadful day when everything went so badly wrong is the same now as then.

Alfred must, I think, have been a contented man in the ninth decade of his life. He looks back to his childhood and early working experiences with great pleasure and satisfaction. For Alfred, the past is a good place. His family is happy and loving – his mother is kind, his father is hard working and respected in the village. Somerset's summer skies are always blue and its winter landscape glitters white with frost. The Mendip Hills are endlessly beautiful and the tumbling streams are crystal clear. His pals at school are boisterous and fun-loving, like small boys should be. When he goes to work at the big house, the cheerful maids treat him like their favoured little brother and the butler turns out to have a Jeeves-esque range of endearing hidden talents. When his GWR apprenticeship calls for him to move away from home, his landlady is motherly and his stationmaster proves to be a wise and benevolent man.

Nevertheless, the general sunniness of Alfred's memories does not mean that he shies away from reality. Hard times are never far away. His grandfather and grandmother have lived the latter part of their adult lives staving off the threat of the workhouse and one summer's day an appalling tragedy befalls a neighbouring family. Although most of the people in Alfred's story are decent, straightforward folk, he also recognises that there are bad people in the world as well as good. Indeed, we meet one of the former type almost immediately in the looming form of 'Schoolmaster' and his 'dreaded stick'.

Alfred's own experiences are not always easy. Childhood comes to a juddering halt when he turns 12 and, in exchange for an annual wage of £3 plus meals, he must immediately begin working morning 'till night, seven days a week as a servant at the home of one of the two local 'squires'. Four years later, a tough, physical environment awaits him when, still no more than a boy, he moves on to join the railway.

Alfred rarely seems deterred, however. His hardworking adolescence was, of course, no different from that of other lads around him – and easier than some – but from our twenty-first-century perspective we can only be surprised at the equanimity with which he describes the demands and privations of these boyhood years. If anything, the nature of his employment seems to inspire a sense of identity and belonging and he feels loyalty and some affection towards the wealthy family for whom he works as a servant. Later, when he moves on to the GWR, he quickly begins to see himself as a small but valuable part in a great and admirable enterprise. He adores the GWR's great locomotives with their gleaming paint and polished brass and he loves the majestic way the tracks sweep across the countryside from London to Bristol and beyond.

So far, I have tried to give a sense of the entertainment value of the memoir, but its qualities go further than that. It is engaging because of the light it shines on the forgotten detail of nineteenth-century life. It describes a rural school from the point of view of a child and 'downstairs' life at the home of the local squire from the point of view of the lad at the bottom of the pecking order. It recalls an age of deference to, in Alfred's words, 'the Quality'. For Alfred, son of a servant and destined to begin his own working life as a servant, this idea of innate difference between the social classes is imbued with an absolute sense of permanence. Yet, as we now know, unquestioned deference of this kind would begin to dissolve before Alfred even reached middle age.

The memoir also describes a rural life that had remained unchanged for generations but which was now sliced through by that most modern of developments – and one of the leading characters in Alfred's story – the national railway system. By the time Alfred was born the railway was well on the way to putting more or less everywhere in reach of more or less everywhere else. The villages of the Mendips may have been, like much of the rest of the West Country, remote from London and the thriving industrial cities of the Midlands and the North where the majority now lived, but they were no longer cut off (even tiny Langford, which had no station during Alfred's childhood, was to gain one in 1901).

Alfred's memories of the GWR have a similar sense of inviting us to rub off the dust and peer in through the leaded glass. There exists an extensive literature on the history of railways in Britain, but Alfred's story is not about technical developments in locomotives and rolling stock, nor is it about audacious civil-engineering projects. Alfred draws our attention to something much more modest – the relationship between the railway and the day-to-day life of rural communities. The memoir suggests that by the late nineteenth century, railway stations had settled into place in the countryside without any drama, like a prosperous but considerate uncle slipping quietly into a family party so as not to upstage the host. In Alfred's memoir, these small centres of activity, busy with produce and packages as well as passengers, are seen to have become as much a part of the fabric of village life as the church, the school and the pub.

Alfred himself was taken away from the old life by the railway but he remained a West Country working man, and the presence of that authentic and under-represented voice in the memoir is the final reason in my list of reasons why the memoir deserves to be made more widely available. There is no way of knowing whether Alfred intended his memoir for public consumption. His fictionalising of the names of people and places suggests that that he may, perhaps, have hoped that it had the potential to be published; if so, I am delighted to have helped bring that about for him – albeit sixty years after his death. But even if it was never intended for eyes other than those of his friends and family, I am confident the memoir merits a wider audience and I hope Alfred would be pleased.

Apart from correcting a couple of dozen typing errors and the small number of spelling mistakes that were present, I have interfered with Alfred's original text in only two ways. The first is that I have amended the punctuation where necessary to improve the readability; in particular, Alfred had a slight tendency to write long sentences linked with several 'ands'. Where that was the case I have split the long sentence into two or three shorter ones. The second change that I have made is rather more complicated and I explain it in the following paragraphs. Other than these two tweaks to the mechanics of the memoir, every word and every sentence you read are precisely as Alfred originally wrote them.

As I mentioned at the outset, the memoir was written anonymously. As well as hiding his own identity, Alfred also keeps from the reader the real names of almost all the other people about whom he writes. This doesn't matter quite so much in the second half of the memoir once Alfred has left home to work for the GWR, but it is of more consequence in the first half, where people and the connections between them are a fundamental part of the story. Apart from referring to his father by name a couple of times, Alfred uses no names at all for his own family, choosing instead to say 'my brother', 'my sister', 'my grandfather' and so on. He also refrains from naming the wealthy families for whom he and his father worked. For these people, he again prefers generic terms such as 'the squire', 'my lady', 'my lady's mother'. At no point, either, does he identify the grand houses in which they lived.

Clearly this was all a conscious decision on Alfred's part. He wanted to tell his story but, at the same time, he wanted to respect the privacy of his family and to exercise discretion in relation to the local gentry who formed such an important part of childhood experience. Once I had identified Alfred, I was able to use the family history resources that are now available online (census records, birth, marriage and death registrations and so on) to put together the details of his family. That was fairly easy. It took rather longer to identify the two land-owning local families around whom Alfred's early family story revolves. Luckily, Alfred had mentioned some physical details of the houses that I was able to check against old photographs. Also helpful were a handful of observations about the blood relationships between the families. Once I had confidently put names to the families concerned, I was able to use the public record to assemble the complete picture. Wealthy families like those in Alfred's story tend to be much more thoroughly documented than working-class families like his own.

Incidentally, Alfred's deep-rooted respect for the rural aristocracy does not blind him to their failings and foibles. There is an entertaining sprinkling of frankness in his storytelling. No family secrets are given away and no scandals are exposed but Alfred feels justified in forming an opinion. He does not hesitate roundly to disparage one particular individual who, on the evidence of her imperious behaviour, seems thoroughly to deserve it.

Beyond the land-owning gentry, I was occasionally able to identify other people in the story by using public records. To take one example, I was able to track down the rather splendid name of Alfred's first stationmaster at the GWR, one Emanuel Day. Once these various 'characters' had their real names, it seemed to make sense, just here and there and where it felt appropriate, to insert those names into the text instead of sticking with the impersonal nouns used by Alfred. This has, I think, given a pleasing sense of identity to the people concerned and made the text read more naturally. Whenever you read a full name (i.e. forename and surname together) it will, in all but two or three cases, have been inserted into the text by me. Very occasionally, Alfred himself uses a full name but in only one of those cases have I been able to verify that as a real name. That example, Alfred's friend Will Came who goes off to join the army, is noted in the endnotes.

For similar reasons to those above, I have also used the real names of the two large houses and restored the real names of the villages whose names Alfred had fictionalised. This latter was very easy to do, since Alfred's made-up names turned out to be unmistakeable near-approximations of the real names. To take, as an example, the two that appear most frequently, Alfred had replaced Langford with 'Linford' and Burrington with 'Brinton'. From Alfred's GWR work records and the 1891 census record, I was also able to identify the village of Worle to which he moved in order to take up his new job at the local station. Every place name that appears in the book is now a real name and in every case has been inserted into Alfred's original sentences by me.

On a broader scale, I have, in a number of places, moved sections of the text around. In the original, Alfred sometimes writes about something just when he is reminded of it by something else. For example, just after he has described his first visit to Bristol as a small boy, he goes on to describe the outing to the Bristol pantomime paid for by 'my lady' for the staff of the big house. This leads him on to a description of the later and rather ill-fated visit he and his pal, Sam, made to Bristol Docks. This way of writing works perfectly well in the conversational style of the memoir but would, I think, have seemed illogical at times in this book. In the particular example given above, as in other similar cases, I have taken the incidents concerned and placed them chronologically. In order to make the memoir fit within the space constraints of the book, it has also been necessary to edit the memoir down to around three-quarters of its original size.

I have had lots of help in finding photographs to accompany the text. The local history societies in both of the villages that feature in the book have been enthusiastic in their support for my project, as have the two most important archives of material relating to the GWR. My gratitude is properly expressed on the acknowledgements page but inevitably, even with this expert help, it has not been possible on every occasion to find relevant photographs from the exact period of Alfred's memoir. I've been pleased with the range of photographs that people were able to turn up for me and I have always used the photographs nearest in time to the period of the memoir. Most photographs are from within twenty-five years or so of the period of the memoir but in some cases – for example the photographs of Worle Station – the only photographs available are from some decades later. Where a photograph is from a different period, it is explained in the caption.

The photographic Holy Grail would, of course, have been a picture of Alfred himself but, despite my trying several different routes, I was not able to track one down. This is undoubtedly a disappointment but, on the plus side, it does mean that you, like me, have the pleasure of being able to conjure up an Alfred Plumley entirely to your own specifications. One tiny but tangible connection to the real Alfred did come my way during the writing of this book. The pleasing coincidence by which that happened is described in the epilogue.

So what has been my own contribution, apart from the editing of Alfred's memoir and the research to identify the real people and places involved?

Well, I could see that there were a number of places in the memoir where it would helpful to add short sections explaining the historical context for events that happen. A small but typical example of this occurs quite early in the book when Alfred describes the arrangements for his schooling. It is useful, I think, to understand that Alfred's parents had to pay a small weekly fee because fully state-funded schooling was not yet established in Britain. Similarly, it is interesting to know that when Alfred was aged 6 or 7, compulsory school attendance (up to the age of 12) was introduced nationwide for the first time. In other words, Alfred happened to be a small boy during the precise years that education provision in Britain first took the form that it still has today. These historical changes undoubtedly had a bearing on the life chances that later came Alfred's way, including, probably, his ability in old age to write a memoir.

In addition to this contextual information, I have occasionally added short linking paragraphs as Alfred moves from one part of the memoir to another. My contributions to the text of chapters 1, 2 and 3, where Alfred's memoirs are laid out, can be clearly identified by use of a lighter text and a dotted line. This method of differentiating my words from Alfred's will enable you to skip the background information, if you wish.

My other contribution has been to add explanatory endnotes in relation to those obscure words and long-forgotten details of everyday life that turn up in all vernacular writing. These notes are at the end of the book along with references to the source of some of the historical information I have added. I have tried to make these endnotes as entertaining as possible and I hope they will enhance your enjoyment of the book. In the later part of the book I have also aimed to pay due respect to the epic undertaking that was the GWR by sketching in enough detail to interest those who know little about nineteenth-century railways without patronising those who already know a lot.

I have tried to make my own contributions unobtrusive. My intention in adding them at all – if I can enter into the spirit of the thing by ending this introduction with a railway analogy – has been only to make sure that the timetables are correct, the announcements audible and that there is a smartly uniformed chap on the platform to point you in the right direction. In other words, I have tried to create the simplest possible framework for the greatest enjoyment of Alfred's original words. I hope you have a pleasant journey.

Family and Circumstances, 1879

Alfred

Alfred Plumley was born on 6 July 1874. His memoir begins in 1879 when he is 5 years old. He lives with his father, mother and two brothers in the village of Lower Langford, Somerset.

Lower Langford

Lower Langford is situated on the western edge of the picturesque Mendip Hills, 12 miles south of Bristol and 10 miles east of Weston-super-Mare. The area is rural and the landscape is hilly, with limestone outcrops, caves and gorges. The area was (and remains) relatively sparsely populated, with most people living in small villages. The largest town in the western Mendips, Cheddar, still has a population of fewer than 6,000. At the end of the nineteenth century, the period that Alfred recalls in his memoir, most working people in Lower Langford and the surrounding villages worked in agriculture, lead mining, quarrying or, like the Plumley family, were in service.

Freddy and Mary Plumley

At the opening of the memoir, Alfred's father, Charles Frederick Plumley (known as Freddy), is 33. Freddy was born and brought up in the nearby village of Burrington. Alfred's mother, Mary, is a year older than her husband. Mary may have been Welsh, since Alfred tells us she was raised in an orphanage in Swansea, both of her parents having died when she was a little girl.

Edward, William and Kate Plumley

Alfred's older brother, Edward, is aged 8 when the memoir opens. Alfred's younger brother, Ernest William (known by his middle name), is not yet a year old. Alfred's sister, Catherine (known as Kate), will be born when Alfred is 9, in 1883. Birth records for the locality suggest that Freddy and Mary may have had four other children between 1870 and 1877, all of whom died in their first year of life. None of these babies is mentioned in Alfred's memoir.

Charles and Ann Plumley

Alfred's paternal grandparents, Charles and Ann Plumley, live in the neighbouring village of Upper Langford. Earlier in life, Charles had worked as an agricultural labourer but a serious accident involving an overturned cart had left him disabled. He and Ann have since lived in very poor circumstances.

Langford Court and the lodge cottage

The Plumley family lives in the lodge cottage belonging to Langford Court. Langford Court is a substantial seventeenth-century manor house surrounded by parkland and estate. Rent-free residence at the lodge is a benefit of Freddy's job. He works as coachman to the owner of Langford Court, Evan Henry Llewellyn. Langford Court still exists. It remains a private residence.

'Squire', his family and his household

Evan Llewellyn is referred to in Alfred's memoir simply as 'Squire'. In 1879 Evan is 33 years old. He gives his occupation in the 1881 census as Justice of the Peace. During the course of the memoir he will be elected as Conservative MP for North Somerset (he is also, incidentally, great-grandfather to the former prime minster, David Cameron). Evan lives with his wife Mary and their six young children (their seventh and final child will be born subsequently). Mary Llewellyn was born locally and is a member of the Somers family, an established family of local landowners. In 1881, Langford Court has a resident household staff of eight plus a number of other servants and outdoor staff who live out.

Work and status

The lodge where the Plumley family lives functions as the gatehouse to Langford Court. In addition to keeping house and caring for her young family, Mary Plumley is expected, in Alfred's words, 'always to be at home and on the alert to open the big iron gates to allow the squire or any of his visitors to ride or drive through'. Because the position of coachman to the squire is an important one, the Plumley family is relatively well off by local standards. Freddy Plumley earns 18s a week, which makes him, as Mary proudly reminds the children from time to time, 'about the best paid man in the village'.[1]

Langford Court, Lower Langford, Somerset, home of 'Squire' (Evan Henry Llewellyn). The Plumley family lived in the gatehouse to Langford Court. Langford Court still stands and is largely unchanged in appearance, but the gatehouse was demolished many years ago and it was not possible to find a photograph of it. (Post 1890, Stan Croker Collection)

1

Alfred Plumley

Schoolboy

Village schooldays

At five years of age I started one fine morning in the summer on the two mile walk to school. I did not want to go but my elder brother, Edward, having tight hold of my right hand and going that way himself, I just had to trot along beside him.

Now in those days it was a common practice for mothers to tell a fractious boy that if he wasn't good an old man would put him in a sack and take him off. We had done most of our journey when, round a bend of the road, came the very old man himself. As soon as I saw him I knew he was the real old bogie-man, for he had the big sack on his shoulder very plain to be seen.

Snatching my hand away from my brother's, I let out a yell and started back homewards as fast as my little legs would carry me but I didn't get far. My brother overtook me and pinned me down on the roadside till the old chap shuffled by. I well remember how, in passing, he smiled down at me and said, 'I wouldn't hurt 'ee, my little man.' He looked so kind that I was never frightened of the old man with the sack after that.

In spite of this hold up we reached Burrington Church of England School in good time and I was put on the Infants' Class Register. This cost my parents 3*d* a week 'School Money'.[1] The school was considered the best for miles around and several farmers living in other parishes sent their children there in preference to schools nearer home. Some children arrived in pony traps or on donkeys, getting stabling for the animals in the outbuildings of a nearby farmhouse.

Although they would not have known, as they trotted off down the lane to school on that sunny summer morning, Alfred and Edward were among the very earliest of British children to benefit from a nationally organised education system.

Political fears about artificially closing the gap between the social classes and worries about losing child labour from industry and agriculture meant that nineteenth-century Britain had lagged behind other developed countries in establishing a state education system. As a result, in almost every part of the country, churches and charitable institutions had stepped into the breach, opening independent elementary schools to serve their own local area. These schools – voluntary schools, as they were known – offered a basic education that was not free but was priced to be affordable for most. By the 1860s, there was a voluntary school within reach of the majority of the population. Burrington Primary was founded as a voluntary school by the local church in 1854.

The 1870 Education Act took the first steps toward a national education system by allowing local communities to set up 'School Boards'. School Boards were public bodies allowed to levy a rate to support existing voluntary schools or set up new schools. A School Board was set up in Burrington sometime around the date that Alfred started school (the precise date seems not to be known). In a further development, the 1880 Education Act, whose provisions came into force during Alfred's first year at school, made school attendance compulsory for the first time.

Local schools were far from perfect during these early years but it is true to say that little Alfred was present at the birth of an educational system recognisable as the earliest ancestor of the one we still have today. It is difficult now to imagine just what an absolutely radical social change it was when education first became available to all children, regardless of where they lived or their parents' ability to pay – although, as Alfred's memoir reminds us, in rural areas the new system was introduced against the background of a way of life where change was otherwise very slow in coming.

Burrington Church of England School, adjoining Burrington Church. Both buildings are more or less unchanged to the present day. (Post 1890, Stan Croker Collection)

In my early days at school I well remember the sound of flails beating out the grain in a threshing shed so close to the school that we always knew when this business was on by the monotonous thumps.[2] One playtime I went up a short flight of steps to an open door and watched the men sitting on the floor wielding their flails up, over and down. Two winnowing machines were installed there to carry on the process – long box-like affairs fitted with fans operated by handles which on being turned threw the refuse away from the grains.

One day when I passed by a big cloud of chaff blew all over me. A man was shovelling the sweepings out of a door about eight feet from the ground. A good steady breeze was blowing which carried the refuse away and grain among it fell on a sheet spread below, nothing much in it I guess but in those days every bit of grain was chased around. This was about 1880 and I think steam threshing machinery was in fairly common use. I expect this small threshing floor was owned by a man who was determined to stick to his ancestor's methods to the last.

For many country children like Alfred, the new system of compulsory schooling meant there was no avoiding a long trek in all weathers to get to school and back. Despite the fact that walking long distances was much more a part of everyday life then than it is now, the journey to and from school must still have been an ordeal at times. In the winter, particularly, many children would have lacked warm clothes and decent shoes. Reliable waterproof clothing had yet to be invented. As Alfred recalls, some children had to go without food all day too. Even summer days could be a problem, as Alfred describes.

Many of us, had to walk several miles to school and in the hot summer months it was very difficult to get a drink of water. During the winter and early spring, water would be flowing from a pipe projecting from the roadside bank but when water was so badly needed in the hot summer months, this source would be dried up. A little old lady who kept a small shop nearby would sometimes allow us to get water from her well. The water level in the well was normally about forty feet down. A heavy iron-hooped bucket attached to a winch was wound up and down to provide the clear cool water so much desired by us lads.

It took two of us to turn the handle to raise the bucket when it was full, then, when it was near the top, if one lad was silly enough to let go of the winch handle to grab at the bucket – and miss – the other lad couldn't hold it and down the well the heavy bucket would return making the winch handle revolve at a tremendous rate. It would strike the water with a great splash and for a day or two the water would be too thick to drink. There would be a stampede away, for the old lady would rush out shrieking at us and we all felt a little afraid of her. I had even heard it whispered that she was a witch but I'm sure she was a good old soul, for after a few days when some of us, driven by thirst, ventured to approach her again, she never refused us.

While I was attending school, a fine modern iron pump was erected close by and for a month or so one could get water from it, then it refused to function and never did again in my time though it was allowed to stand there rusting away. We lads used often to bang the heavy iron handle up and down with no good result. Many of us would have given our best alley marble for a drink.

There was a lot of poverty about among the working classes in those days and if father was out of work many a boy attending school could bring little or nothing with him to eat when dinner time came round. We lads who were better supplied had to look keenly after our 'tommy bags' or the dinners meant for us would be missing – gone to fill the tummy of a near starving schoolmate.[3] If one of us found our bag empty there was nothing for it but to beg a bite or two from a special mate, just enough to keep one alive until he reached home about 5.00 p.m.

An authoritarian regime

With the other little nippers of my age I worked through the Infants' Class Room, two Lower Standard Rooms and reached the Main Room, over which the schoolmaster exercised constant personal supervision and where I soon found out what a tyrant he was. Very rarely was the rod of correction out of his hand. There was no fancy cane for him - any old hedge stick would do. Later I was sent out several times to get one for him from a nearby hedge. When he brought it down on an unlucky child's hand a white weal would soon appear. If the little hand was not held out horizontally, he would apply the stick to the under part with an upward flick so that he could make good contact on the downward stroke.

I marvel that many little hands were not crippled for life by the severe strokes. Having a real dread of Schoolmaster's stick and being pretty good at my lessons I received much less punishment than the average but no boy escaped entirely. From the occasional doses I had, I can assure you that Schoolmaster's method of turning out a good scholar was very painful to the scholar.

There was a great commotion one day, for one of the biggest boys on receiving an unexpected blow from him when in class, made a show of retaliating and we 'tiddlers' looked on horrified at the punishment he received. Mind you, Schoolmaster was no feeble old man but about at his best and a good athlete. That boy must have been covered with weals and bruises. For a half hour or more he just lay on the floor sobbing. Schoolmaster was so heated and agitated that he left the room to recover his composure. I never heard that the lad's parents made any complaint to the authorities – but then Schoolmaster was a very important man in the parish.

Of course, we had home lessons to cope with and in those days pen and ink was not to be found in many cottages. The lessons were generally geography. Each scholar in the upper classes had to buy a two-penny geography book from Schoolmaster and a certain country was selected for every evening's study. We had to memorise the chief towns, principal imports, exports, fairs, climate, rivers, mountains and boundaries. For big countries such as Russia or America we might be allowed two evenings or even three. Then each morning, after prayers, Schoolmaster, stick in hand, would put questions to each lad to ascertain if he had spent part of the previous evening in study. Every morning several lads would feel the sting of his stick.

We were also taught grammar but during my schooldays I never understood why, for it was never explained to us how necessary it was to enable one to speak or write correctly and I regarded it merely as another task that had to be worried through. I was always good with the pen though and was very proud of my copybook but lost a lot of my zeal when Schoolmaster told me to stop in part of dinner time to superintend the efforts of a number of poor writers who had a lesson set them as a punishment. He had the idea I should feel honoured. No fear. I wanted liberty, fresh air and, above all, my dinner – first bite of anything since an eight o'clock breakfast.

As I got older, Schoolmaster singled me out to do many little jobs not included in the school curriculum. Sometimes, with the help of another boy, I'd be told off to weed his garden path – fortunately a very short one. Occasionally I would be sent off to an absent boy's home to ascertain why he was not at school and the usual excuse was, 'His boots are gone to be mended and he can't come till we get 'em back.' This was a perfectly valid excuse as many boys owned only one pair.[4]

One outstanding job sticks in my memory. With another boy I was ordered to burn up a score or more of old dog-eared Bibles. No easy job, for we had no material with which to start a good fire and consequently had to tear up the books before we could dispose of them. I nearly mutinied over this job for it didn't seem right to me. Our family Bible was always handled so reverently at home that I worried over this act of desecration for months.

Village rivalry – and Alfred has an accident

A strong wave of militarism pervaded our school one year when I was about eight. Every boy recruited was expected to provide himself with a light wooden sword, usually a length of lath with a short crosswise piece near the hilt. Heavy weapons were taboo. We didn't want fatalities – minor casualties and the rout of the enemy sufficed.

Our weapons would be hidden in a bush or hedgerow during school hours from which they could be quickly recovered when lessons were over. One day a farmer's son showed up with a real sword – a relic of his father's yeomanry days. He had smuggled it out of his home and after he had allowed a few of us to handle it and the younger recruits to admire it, he had to smuggle it back home. This wanted some doing, for you couldn't put a thing that size in your pocket!

I believe Schoolmaster got to hear of this real weapon having been in our hands for, a day or so after, he gave out strict orders that all hostilities had to cease and every boy to go straight home after dismissal from school. We Langford boys recovered our weapons and obeyed but had only gone about a quarter of a mile before we were attacked in the rear by a strong force of the enemy from Burrington and Rickford.

It was unthinkable that we should run, so we faced about and joined battle. At it we went hammer and tongs and I guess we'd have won but just at the crisis Schoolmaster came rushing into the fray like a modern tank going into action. Casualties were numerous. I was on the right flank of our army and instead of joining in the general rout, rushed away unnoticed on my own and hid up in a thick hedge quite near, where I had a good view of the stricken field.

Schoolmaster just ran among the fleeing boys, dealing out blows and pushes with both hands. Over they went like falling ninepins – but we were tough lads in those days and there were no stretcher cases and soon every warrior was going soberly home.

Schoolmaster walked off in a far different manner than how he arrived and I came out of the hedge the most unruffled of the lot. Had I been witnessing a real battle I could have sent off a full report to the press. But the matter didn't finish here. Next morning, after that old hypocrite had led us in prayers, we bigger boys were lined up. The Burrington and Rickford boys with both hands outstretched had a good whack on each. We

31

Children pose in the lane leading to Burrington School. (Post 1890, Stan Croker Collection)

Langford boys got off with one, a remission to us because we were actually on our way home. This brought to an end all our military exercises and we returned to more peaceful games such as rounders, 'duckey', 'warney', 'catty' and suchlike.[5]

One Christmas holiday I had a bit of bad luck. Several of us boys had a good long slide across a big pond that was hard frozen. As I was gliding down it I fell heavily backwards, the back of head meeting the ice first. Concussion, I reckon. I had a very dim idea of being dragged away into the grass on the side and there I was left until my mates saw fit to go home.

On returning to school a few days later our class was soon lined up for mental arithmetic, a favourite subject with our schoolmaster and one in which I excelled but now I was just hopeless at it – and have been ever since. Schoolmaster barked at me, 'Whatever is the matter with you?' No time for an explanation, I had to drift to the bottom of the class and stay there.

Church and choir

Schoolmaster was very keen on music and singing, played the church organ at all services and trained the choir. I detested singing and was in the habit of opening and shutting my mouth in unison with the others but did not contribute one bit to the melody. I was doing my share in this way one afternoon when I received a blow on the back that should have broken the spinal column. That snooper of a schoolmaster had crept round behind me and this was his playful way of letting me know he had rumbled to the fact that I wasn't squeaking away like the others.

After that I was bound to try and I succeeded so well that I was selected to join the church choir where I did a few months' chirping but was so irregular in attendance on practice nights that Schoolmaster told me if I stayed away again I should stay away altogether. This remark I gladly accepted as demobilisation and at the next Sunday morning service I was sitting in a pew with several of my school mates.

Sam Purnell sat next to me and during the long sermon Sam fell fast asleep. Parson was droning away when, with a loud explosive 'Oh!' Sam sprang a foot and a half up from his seat. Parson stopped his sermon and everyone turned their heads in our direction. Verger approached in a stealthy deliberate manner, took hold of Sam by his nearest ear and leading him down the aisle, opened the church door and thrust Sam out – not into outer darkness but into the sunshine of a fine summer day.

I wished I was with him but I didn't favour his method of departure and wasn't I relieved to see Verger retire to his seat for my ears sensed he might return for another culprit as he must have known that poor Sam didn't himself fire the rocket that hoisted him up in the air? Of course, it was that rascal sitting on the other side of him. He drove a pin well and truly into Sam's 'sit-upon' and caused all the trouble.

Only Sunday School children were invited to the parson's tea-party. Parson and his plump little wife used to be buzzing around us all through the afternoon arranging races and games of various sorts. He would bring out his bowls and jack and give the bigger lads an insight into the game. There would be several big vessels containing about four inches of water, many pennies and an occasional silver three-penny bit, the coins having to be taken out by the lips. It was no easy job to make a fortune that way.

Later in the year there was a Choir Supper. I was never eligible but once. This was a posh affair. Parson and his wife sat at table with us and we had a sumptuous feast, being waited on by the maidservants, after which old and young engaged in various games such as 'Hunt the Slipper', 'Postman's Knock', 'Truckle the Trencher', 'Consequences', etc.[6]

Alfred's mum and dad make an entrance

One afternoon at school, very soon after our dinner break, our tyrant of a dominie[7] happened to see me whisper to my nearest classmate and immediately ordered me to go to a small side-room and wait till he came. Now, as I have previously stated, I had a perfect horror of corporal punishment as administered by him and after being shut up in this room by myself for what seemed half a day, I got into a very nervous condition. Then, strange to say, a sentence in the morning scripture lesson – 'Let not your heart be troubled' – came vividly to my memory and I had hardly digested the comfort of those few words when the door was opened by a teacher who said, 'You are wanted.' I followed her out to the school porch. There was that dreaded old schoolmaster talking ever so courteously to my mother, Mary, who at once took hold of my hand and said 'Come along.' Go! I was free!

As mother hurried me off she told me Squire had given my dad, Freddy, the afternoon off and the use of a horse and trap to take us to a sheep-shearing match held in a village about six miles distant, for he knew how interested father was in sheep. I was not a bit concerned about the sheep but wasn't I relieved to escape the punishment I expected and to be enjoying a ride over fresh country behind a fine fast horse in my parents' company?

Freddy and Mary

My father was a devout man and it was our usual custom on a Sunday evening for the whole family to sit around the table with our open Bibles and to read a verse each in turn from chapters selected by father. He was never a demonstrative man and I never knew him to air his views in public. I am sure he was very popular in the village; blacksmith, innkeeper, carpenter and other village worthies of about his own age always addressed him as 'Freddy' and all lesser folk tacked on the 'Mr'.

How he learned to read and write I could never find out for he said he never went to school. Anyhow, he could do both when it was common to meet men of his age in those days who could do neither. A walk round the garden in the spring and a look at his neatly written labels on the seed beds showed he could write and when the weekly newspaper was delivered every Saturday evening, he was keen to get hold of it and would read out any striking news to any of the family present. I never knew him to write but one letter in his life and that was to my elder brother, the first to leave the nest for the outside world. Edward treasured that missive till he died at the age of seventy-five, then it came into my possession.

With such an upbringing it was not to be wondered at that we boys always got full marks for scripture knowledge, first class Diocesan Certificates and many book prizes. One year I had a full-sized *Robinson Crusoe*, profusely illustrated. I just revelled in this most suitable book for boys. We had cards, draughts and dominoes to amuse us in the long winter evenings. Sometimes we visited our neighbours for games and sometimes they came to us.

Father could drink his glass of beer or tot of whisky as well as the next man but I don't believe he ever spent an hour in a public house in his life and never took more than was good for him – but he came perilously near one evening. He had taken the squire in his carriage to a political meeting and mother let us youngsters stay up a bit later than usual to keep her company. She would read to us or tell us stories on a dark evening such as this was. She was much better educated than the average countrywoman. She wrote a fine hand and read out of a paper or book quite fluently. I never heard her say much about her childhood but I did know that she lost both parents when very young and was brought up in an orphanage in or near

Swansea. No doubt she got a much better education than she would have had otherwise.

Well, there we were listening to mother, all as comfortable as could be wished for, when the door opened and in tottered father in full livery: frock-coat, very tight doeskin breeches and top boots. His face was all lit up and he seemed quite happy as he stuttered out to mother, 'Mary, I've lost all that money.' Mother's face was far from expressing happiness as she stepped up to him and said, 'Where did you have it?' 'In my breeches pocket,' he answered. Instantly, mother pushed her slim hand right down to the bottom of the pocket of those skin tight breeches and I saw a look of relief flash in her face, then an instant after, she withdrew her hand and we saw three golden sovereigns in it. 'There 'tis,' she said.

Father sheepishly said 'Well well', and there was general rejoicing. It seemed that father owed these three sovereigns to a farmer who had delivered several young pigs to us a few days before. He had hoped to see him at the meeting and discharge his debt. Squire was exceedingly popular and of course, his coachman had to be treated – and more than once. In consequence, Dad was really not equal to getting his work-worn hand to the bottom of that deep tight pocket, so he'd concluded he'd lost his money and farmer wasn't paid that evening.

To celebrate Queen Victoria's Jubilee in 1887 several villages combined to organise a fete and sports and by this co-operation it was quite a big event. I was by father's side when the veterans' race was announced. Several of the committee were weaving about amongst the spectators persuading the old chaps to come forward and one old toff came up to father and insisted on his entering. Very much against his inclination, father at last consented. The contestants just took off their coats and lined up – quite a good entry. Then at the bang of the pistol, off they went. A one lap race and to our surprise and jubilation father came along to breast the tape, an easy winner. I had the satisfaction of repeating father's performance in the Peace Celebrations of 1918 but I didn't have as many rivals as he had.

My mother knew the right remedy for all common complaints and many that were not so common. Every spring we youngsters were sent off with a big basket to gather a large quantity of primroses – just the blossoms, no stem or leaves. It seemed a bit hard on those welcome heralds of warmer days but the end justified the means for mother made of these flowers the most soothing and healing ointment you could wish for. Spread on a bit of clean rag and applied to a cut or sore, even a severe one would heal up in a few days. Should an abscess appear one of mother's herbal poultices would draw out the poison and the primrose ointment soon complete a cure.[8]

One day, Edward and I, schoolboys at the time, were in the wood-shed. I was busy chopping up sticks for firewood when my brother came close and put his hand on the chopping block. I asked him to take it off but he only grinned so I said, 'If you don't I'll chop it off.' Thinking he'd be sure to remove it after such a threat, I raised the hook and brought it down – and, to my horror, chopped off the top joint of one of his fingers, except that it was hanging by a bit of skin.

Edward cried out to mother who was close by in the kitchen. I panicked and ran away. That dangling finger top and the blood frightened me so much I pictured myself as a little 'Cain' and was tortured by remorse. It was getting dark before I ventured back home, driven to do so by such an empty little stomach. Mother met me at the door and I'm sure she understood how contrite I felt, for she said, 'Come on in, my son. I think it will be alright.' She had put the finger top back in its place, found suitable bits of wood for splints and bandaged it up as neat and clean as any surgeon could have done. How she ever obtained the knowledge to treat such a case I can't imagine for there were no first aid classes in being round our district but alone and unaided my mother made a successful job of it.

The finger healed up – helped by primrose ointment of course – but was a trifle crooked at the top where the bone had been cut through, not enough to be noticeable unless looked for but up to the time of his death in his seventies, my brother, on our periodic meetings, would hold it up to me and say, 'D'you know who did that?' I knew alright and felt grateful to the Almighty for providing us with such a mother.

Alfred visits Bristol – and doesn't enjoy it

I well remember my first visit to Bristol, though I was very young. I am not sure that I had started school. Father was to take one of Squire's traps to the carriage builders and return with another. He took me with him – just we two – and, it being a nice fine day, I fully enjoyed the ride but the crowded streets of the city made me wonder how we would ever get to the builders or if we should ever be able to get out again if we did.

We were held up in the heart of the city as the drawbridge was up to allow shipping to pass up the river.[9] I was so thrilled to see the tall masts of the passing craft for, young as I was, I had heard of Dick Whittington and Cabot and their adventures abroad, and also of pirates. This seemed to savour of the real thing and surely any boy would experience a thrill at his first sight of a sailing vessel, even if it was only a trading schooner. Before the bridge was lowered there was such a big jumble of many kinds of vehicles waiting to proceed but eventually we crossed the river alright and on our return journey had a clear road.

My next visit to the great city occurred a year or two later in the school holidays. For some reason mother thought a change would be good for my brother and I, so it was arranged that her Aunt Bertha, who lived at Westbury-on-Trym, should meet us in Bristol and have the care of us for a week or so.[10] We two small boys were sent off one fine morning in the carrier's cart and were set down at the 'Hope and Anchor' on Redcliffe Hill. We had a good sized basket with us containing food and a few additional articles of clothing. No-one was on hand to meet us and we sat down on a stone step in front of the pub for what seemed such a long time and I said to my brother, 'What are we going to do if no-one comes for us?' Edward said, 'We'll go back home in the evening same way as we came.'

I didn't like the prospect of squatting there all day but thought Edward's idea of returning home much better than being kidnapped and sent overseas as little slave boys (I had a dim recollection of having heard this had happened in one of the stories my mother had read to us). However, about mid-day a tall old lady suddenly appeared in front of us. 'La! La! Mercy, be you our Mary's two little boys?' My brother assured her we were but it was a haphazard sort of business for us, for we had never seen mother's Aunt Bertha before nor, as far as I knew, had she seen us. However, the old lady shepherded us off and later we arrived at her house safely and after a week there mother arrived to take us back home.

Mother seemed quite at home in Bristol and ushered us in and out of trams – horsed trams they were then. Generally one of the horses had a bell on its collar giving notice of its approach. It was dusk before we left town with our local carrier and I had my first sight of a lamplighter as he ran along the street, stopping for a second before each lamp-post to thrust his torch up through a little trap in the lamp case and light the gas. I was glad to get back home again and the little I had seen of town gave me no wish to live there.

Alfred's grandad and some bad luck on a dilly

My grandparents, Charles and Ann Plumley, were quite elderly before I was born and as I grew into school age they were suffering much hardship. Grandfather had met with an accident when in his prime that left him a cripple for the rest of his life. My earliest recollection of him is as a bent, frail old chap who just managed to potter about on his own premises with the help of a walking stick. He always wore a long frock-coat and a round felt hat, which were never renewed, yet were always in fair condition. Anyone might be excused if they mistook him for an old retired parson. His library consisted of three books only – an illustrated English History, a book about the old heathen gods and the book which every respectable cottager possessed, the Bible. I never saw him reading the two first mentioned but he was very frequently immersed in his big printed Bible.

In spite of his disabilities I never knew him irritable or complaining. He didn't take much notice of his young grandchildren but one day he produced a small wooden snuff-box and gave it to me, saying it once belonged to his grandmother. I remember it quite well for I was surprised to think of a snuff-box being owned by a woman. Strange thing to give to a young schoolboy but I guess he had little else to give. Anyhow, I treasured it and have it now.

Being a man of few words I didn't get much information direct from my grandfather but my father took a pleasure in relating to me any old family history and tales of the countryside. I learned from him how, in his early manhood, Grandfather called no man master but like other men living in that part, he cultivated teasels, kept a flock of sheep, and had a horse and 'dilly'.[11] He also had a good productive garden and orchard, always had a pig or two in the sty, did jobs of hauling and generally managed to make a comfortable living till the unfortunate day when he met with his accident.

The growing and marketing of teasels was quite a big business in the locality at the time of father's boyhood and he told me how grandfather and his neighours used to cut, dry and arrange teasels in 'heads' then, with the loaded dillies plan to travel in company the long, long journey to Manchester, where there was a ready sale for them as they were used for cloth dressing.

The trade in teasels is a little-documented and really quite surprising aspect of rural life in Somerset in earlier centuries. The heads of teasel plants had been used in the woollen industry since the late Middle Ages for combing the finished fabric to raise the nap. Although the woollen industry was largely concentrated in the north of England, particularly in West Yorkshire, the best teasels happened to grow 200 miles away, in just a few places in the south-west of the country. The most important growing area of all was in the northern and western Mendips, where the climate and soil conditions were ideally suited.

The result was a thriving trade in teasel plants between the growers in Somerset and the users in the north of England. Almost all the documentary evidence for the teasel trade comes from records in West Yorkshire.[12] The practical details would have been very much the same though for Charles Plumley and his fellow growers around Langford who, as we shall see, seem to prefer to trade with buyers in Manchester.

It is believed that trade in teasels between Somerset and West Yorkshire had been going on since at least the seventeenth century and quite possibly well before that. By the early eighteenth century, the arrangement was well established and large quantities of teasels were sent regularly to be traded on the West Yorkshire wool markets. Initially, the teasels were used in hand processes but by the nineteenth century, machines known as gigs or gig-mills had been developed to do the same job. These machines had a revolving drum to which the teasels were attached. Huge numbers of teasels were needed to supply these machines.

In the eighteenth century, transport to the main trading centre in Leeds had usually been undertaken by using the navigable waterways, beginning by loading the teasels on to 'trows' at Bristol (trows were local sailing boats used to move goods to and from Bristol along the River Severn). Much of the trade at this time was managed by merchants who bought the teasels at one end and sold them at the other. By the 1840s, however, during the period that

Charles Plumley was a teasel grower, the logistics of the trade had changed. Many Somerset growers had cut out the merchants and were travelling to the north of England to sell their produce themselves.

An account of the teasel trade in a contemporary magazine reported each individual Somerset man as taking a 'single-horse cart-load' of around twenty 'packs' to the north of England. A pack contained 20,000 teasels so each man would have 400,000 teasels on board his cart. The magazine further reported that the 'time required for taking a load of teazles to the Yorkshire market from the north eastern part of Somersetshire is fifteen or sixteen days, including the going and returning'.[13] At a time when there were still only a limited number of engineered roads, this must have been an epic journey to undertake on a small cart pulled by one horse. A contemporary engraving of a loaded dilly suggests that it would probably have been piled several times the height of a man. It would have looked something like a hay wagon at harvest time.[14]

After the middle of the nineteenth century demand for Somerset teasels in the north of England gradually began to decline. This was due partly to a contraction of the woollen industry and partly to changes in import regulations, which meant that it became cheaper to import teasels from abroad. The introduction of improved machinery also contributed to a reduction in the need for teasels. By sometime around the mid 1860s, the centuries-old trade between Somerset and the industrial north had dwindled almost to nothing.

The journey north must have been a risky one in any number of obvious ways, but not least because the dilly cart itself sounds to have been a particularly precarious form of transport. The design of the dilly cart was the direct cause of Charles Plumley's disability.

On passing through a farmyard one day with my father, he pointed to a wreck of what was little more than a long slatted platform on wheels and said, 'There's a dilly. Take a good look at it, you're never likely to see another.' There was no driver's seat on the dilly. The common practice was for the driver to ride on the rear end of one of the shafts and one day when my grandfather was in this position, the horse bolted. Grandfather was thrown off and a wheel passing over his leg broke it. Whoever set it should have been gaoled for his foot turned out at about a right angle; 'half past two' it was derisively called.

Grandfather was no good at any hard work after his accident and it is a mystery how he managed to live for many years after in much the same frugal way he was accustomed to. Somehow, his rent was paid, he and his wife had the necessaries of life and like most cottagers in those times he always had a barrel of cyder 'on tap'. But that cyder didn't keep rheumatism away and for some years before his end at 86 years of age he was sorely troubled by it and his wife was confined to her bed. But for real good, kind neighbours they would probably have had to go to the 'House' [the workhouse], a most dreaded, destination for such an independent couple as they had been in earlier life. My parents did all they could but we lived a good mile apart and mother had four young children to care for and was fully occupied with them and other matters that must be attended to.

Many Sundays as soon as dinner was cooked, I was sent off post haste with a dish of hot dinner for the old couple and it was no pleasure trip, for my tummy was clamouring for its mid-day supply. One day when their kind neighbour went in to see if they were alright, she found the old gentleman dead, seated in his armchair his open Bible on his knees, so that he must have passed away very peacefully.[15]

His funeral was attended by many relatives for, in those days, it was the usual custom for men, women and children to attend the ceremony. There was a fine walnut tree at the bottom of grandfather's garden but we boys were never allowed to go after the walnuts without granfer's permission. It was autumn now and the walnuts were falling. While the folk were all busy indoors arranging the procession, I slipped down to the walnut tree and filled one of my jacket pockets with nuts. A little later I was following the bier on the half-mile walk to the churchyard and on the way my conscience told me I'd done wrong in taking the nuts without the customary permission. I got so worried about it that before we'd reached journey's end I had got rid of all the nuts by throwing them one or two at a time into the hedgerow, so that there was no evidence of my guilt when we all stood by the graveside.

After the funeral, grandmother was brought to live with us but she was never able to leave her bed so that with grannie and four nippers to look after, my mother never had an hour's freedom.

We had a surprise when we went up in the attic of grandfather's for we found it filled right up with teasels all set up in 'head', very neat and in good dry condition, just ready for market. They must have been stored up there ever since grandfather met with his accident.[16] My father made enquiries as to their value but found there would be no profit in selling them after paying cost of carriage, so we lads were set to work to get them downstairs and out on the 'green' (a large open space in front of the house) and there they made a big roaring bonfire.

It seemed such a pity to wilfully burn the result of so much labour and I reckon grandfather had stored them in the attic hoping for a return of good market prices. But modern methods at the cloth mills had knocked the bottom out of the teasel trade, never to return.[17]

A few good pieces of mahogany furniture, a big four-poster bed, an old sheep's head clock,[18] candle snuffers and a flint-and-tinder box, together with the usual domestic crockery and cutlery were all the worldly goods the old folk owned. The sheep had all been sold and the orchard let to a neighbour a year or two previously. My father brought home a few chairs and a few bits of china and I think the rest was left in the cottage by arrangement with the next door family who had been so very kind to the old helpless couple and who were taking over the tenancy of the house.

I'm afraid I felt little sorrow at grandfather's death, for during the last few months of his life I had frequently to go to the doctor's surgery, four miles away, to get medicine before attending school. Of course, this made me late for lessons but I was excused owing to the urgency of the task.

Village characters

On a handful of occasions, Alfred's memoir takes a short break from the narrative of his childhood and adolescence to digress into some particular aspect or other of daily life at that time. This is the first of those digressions. In this section, Alfred describes some of the village 'characters' he encountered during the years in which he was growing up.

These are people who made a strong enough impression on Alfred still to be remembered seventy years later. In most cases, it is a peculiarity of behaviour

43

or appearance that has rendered them vivid. The frank stare of the small boy is still present in these memories of Alfred's. This occasionally makes for slightly squeamish reading in a contemporary world where sensitivities about difference and disability are high on the public agenda, but it is interesting to look back at a time when that was not the case. It is also interesting also to see that, in a world where there were no support or care services, 'oddity' seems, on the whole, more likely to have elicited acceptance from the community than intolerance – although Alfred does also describe incidents in which people are bullied or treated unkindly.

I had a surprise one afternoon when walking along a path near the church. On one side was a high bank and reclining on it was such a strange looking old man. He wore a long frock-coat, very baggy trousers and on his head was an old top-hat with about a dozen little paper flags stuck in the band. His face was wreathed in smiles and as I drew near, he extended his left hand – a walking stick was in his right – and said, 'Help me up sonny.' I caught hold and pulled away and after many grunts the old chap managed to get on his feet, where he looked stranger than ever.

His bulky legs resembled those of an elephant and he moved them in the same deliberate manner as we walked together to the main road where he said he would be 'picked up'. I gathered from his chatter that he had come from a village about three miles away in a neighbour's cart and was put out near where I found him so that he might visit our church. I hope the cart did call for the old chap or he would hardly have reached home that night by walking.

When I told our family about him that evening, my dad said, 'That was old Billy Mead, poor chap. He's "not quite the thing". He weighs twenty stone and blows the organ for all services in Churchill church.' It was said that Billy was leaving after the service one Sunday morning when the lady organist passed him. Billy said, 'We made some nice music for 'em this morning, miss.' 'Oh, but you didn't make the music Billy, I did that,' said the lady. Billy was too astonished to reply.

The following Sunday the service started as usual, Billy working the bellows same as he'd done for years and keeping the organ well supplied but when it came to the second verse of the first hymn, the music faded out. Billy wasn't working.

'Go on, Billy,' said the organist in an urgent whisper.

'Now who makes the music Miss?' said Billy.

'Oh, go on, Billy,' pleaded the worried lady.

'Ah, but who makes the music?' repeated Billy.

'Oh, you do, Billy.'

That was all Billy wanted. He'd won. The organ burst into life again.

Granny Burden was a well-known character who was in demand as midwife in most of the cottages to see to the welfare of mother and the safe arrival of the little bit of humanity into the world – and a dear old soul she was. I had a younger brother, William, and sister, Kate, born when I was a boy, so we had Granny in our house for several weeks and I always regarded her as a real granny after those events.

The dear old lady attended at births as long as her strength allowed her. In fact, she had to keep out of the 'House' for she lost her husband in early life and her only son rarely visited her and when he did it was for the sole object of coaxing or bullying a shilling out of her to spend on beer. A real bad lot, he was.

Granny had a gold lustre teapot which was always kept bright and shining on a high shelf. As a wee boy it always attracted me and Granny said several times I should have it one day. I grew up and left the village and forgot all about the teapot. Some time later, when I came home on a weekend, mother told me that Granny had passed away and that a few days before the end, she remembered her promises to me about the 'gold teapot'. Mother was to take it in her keeping for me. Bless her kind heart to remember in her extremity the promises made to a small boy years before. The teapot has been on my top shelf ever since I have had a home and is now.

Sad to say, we had more than our share of feeble-minded folk in the village. One worthy couple had three children, all mentally deficient. The children lived at home with their parents. They were two girls and a boy. The girls were never seen away from their doorstep but the boy was nearly always roaming about the village. They never attended school although the oldest must have been in her teens before the family left our village to live in a remote cottage up on the edge of the hills.

Roger was another. A middle aged man when I was schoolboy, he had only one useful eye. I was told he lost the sight of the other in his youth by the

A scene in the centre of the village of Lower Langford. (Post 1890, Stan Croker Collection)

action of some fools of workmen for, as he was passing a building site, these men threw some lime at him causing blindness of one eye and weakening the other. The poor man depended on the trifle earned by running errands and doing a bit of light gardening. Roger had an unusually big mouth and some of the 'young bloods' of the village had a habit of tossing pennies at him which he was allowed to keep if he caught them in his mouth. Granny Burden mothered this poor man till he died. Often when Granny was away on a case, Roger would come to my mother, to ask for a bite of anything she could spare and she always did find the poor man something to stay his hunger.

Another poor ungainly man who lived with his sister in a little cottage near the school was totally irrational. Unless the weather was very bad he would be on the lookout for us boys to be out for play or dinner and always would plead with us to 'play pigs' and if we consented, his long clumsy figure would be after us with whoops of delight. If he succeeded in catching a boy he would press a bit of wood near the boy's neck and say, 'Now you squeak!'

The more and louder the boy squeaked the more would this poor man enjoy himself. He would just roar with laughter. I suppose he imagined himself as killing, a nice little fat porker. I never heard how he came by this idea of a game but he never varied in his zest for it. He was quite gentle and harmless and any bit of a schoolboy could dominate him. I regret to say that sometimes a few of the rougher boys would ill-treat him but he would never retaliate – as he might so easily have done – he would cry and creep off home.

A young man who lived at Burrington always gave anyone he came near a bit of a shock for he had no nose. He lost it before I was old enough to take notice. I was told – and I feel sure it was true – that it was bitten of by a donkey. The rumour was that he was teasing the donkey when it happened. The nose was quite gone and he looked very strange without it. No doubt he was fully conscious of this for he was seldom seen about the village. He spent a pretty solitary life in the fields and outbuildings of the farmer he worked for.

In a little old cottage right on the edge of the hills, an elderly widow lived with a grown up dumb daughter. They kept a lot of poultry and owned a donkey and cart, and every Eastertide they would go round the near villages with a good supply of home-made Easter cakes. The daughter looked after the donkey while her mother called at the cottages. These cakes were delicious, flat and thin, and about the size of a tea saucer. They were comparatively dear and far too dainty for healthy growing children for before one hardly appreciated the flavour it was gone. My mother never bought us but one each and very wise of her. The mother and daughter were always so clean and neat, and were well respected by their neighbours.

Their donkey was so good tempered and obedient that it must have been very well treated. A man living at Burrington bred donkeys and what pretty little animals they are in the early stages. I'm afraid most of them had very hard treatment later in life for their owners generally thought that just any old patch of weedy ground provided good enough pasture for a donkey and I have seen them beaten brutally when they turned stubborn. It's my belief that a donkey treated and fed properly from birth would prove as docile as any pony.

A farmer living near us obtained a donkey for his two schoolboy sons and often a half dozen of us would get this donkey out in a field and take turns – two at a time – riding it. It was a dangerous game, for that donkey had been teased so much that it was really vicious and would kick and bite. One time it slewed round when I was near it and one of its hind hoofs almost skinned my nearside ear. I gave up taking any part in donkey-baiting after that!

Staff from Lower Langford Post Office pose in the village street. (Post 1890, Stan Croker Collection)

Village tradesmen

The nineteenth century was famously a time of rapidly developing consumerism in urban Britain. Novelty and invention pervaded every material aspect of daily life from furniture to clothing to foodstuffs to sports and hobbies. Booming industries produced a seemingly endless supply of consumer goods in new materials with extravagant forms of decoration and finish. Numerous newly developed mechanical devices emerged, clanking and spluttering, from factories and workshops, promising to replace the drudgery of doing things by hand. Yet in the countryside, things went on much as normal. Poorer people in rural areas still could not easily travel more than a few miles, especially in places like the western Mendips where there was, as yet, no railway branch line to connect the villages to the market towns. Good tradesmen were vital contributors to the quality of village life and were respected for their skills.

Our village was very self-contained. There were three general shops, one of which was also the Post Office, then there was a baker, butcher, shoemaker, two carpenters and a blacksmith.

Every boy from five years to nine or thereabouts owned an iron hoop and most girls a wooden one. All other playthings were very scarce. Our iron hoops occasionally got broken and we lads always had our eyes open to find a cast off horse-shoe, for the smith would mend a hoop without the payment of a penny – the recognised charge – if we could hand over a secondhand shoe. But we had to wait sometimes for days before the smith or his apprentice had the leisure to attend to such a trifling job.

A very busy place was the smithy. Horses were numerous and indispensable and with the clip clop of their hooves and the grinding of the vehicle's iron-bound wheels on the rough roadways there was very little risk of being run over. In the long, dark evenings the smith and his assistant would often be working by lamplight and then the sparks flying from the anvil where the new shoes were being beaten into shape would attract us lads for it was like a miniature firework display. We would gather in a little group in the smithy doorway until we were abruptly ordered 'Out of the way!' to let a horse be led in or out.

We lived within a stone's throw of the shoemaker who made and repaired boots and shoes for nearly all the villagers and was so expert at his trade that he often had orders from the gentry for hunting boots of the best quality. At the other end of the scale I've been in his shop and pulled off my hobnailed boots for him to put in a few new nails to replace those I had kicked out. Just a penny job, done while you waited.

Shoemaker had four children, three girls and the youngest, a boy, on whom his parents doted. He was a mischievous little rascal and his father had often to correct him, which he usually did by pulling off a soft felt hat, his everyday wear, and banging it on the boy's shoulders.

At four years old this boy developed a craze for matches and none must be left within his reach or he'd make off with them to set fire to any bit of combustible stuff he could find. Across the road was a yard, common property of two tenants of thatched cottages who also had a thatched pigsty, each just inside the yard gate. One day a big load of straw was unloaded close by the empty pigsties for they and the cottages were in need of repair to the roofs.

One fine summer afternoon the shoemaker was busy at his craft when he became aware of great billows of smoke obscuring everything outside his windows. He went out at once and saw that the smoke was certainly coming from the big heap of straw and the blazing wooden pigsties.

Nothing could be done but stand aside and let it burn out. Shoemaker, his wife and several other women were just doing this when a sudden fear assailed him and turning to his wife he said, 'Where's our young Will?' No reply. He rushed back indoors calling 'Will! Will!' but there was no sound or sign of his son. He returned to the fire and his wife's face revealed that she was suffering from the same fear that he was.

As soon as it was possible to approach near enough he, having provided himself with a long-handled rake, pulled some of the smouldering boards of the pigsty over and then raking about, a small flat object was pulled towards him. He looked closely at it and his doubt was turned to certainty. It was the sole of a little shoe. He knew it at once for his son's, for he had cut it out and stitched the upper to it a few weeks before. The father turned to my mother who had been present from the first, and whispered to her to take his wife home.[19]

When the fire had cooled off sufficiently a few ashes of what had been an active little boy were collected and taken a few days later to the parish churchyard. It was surmised that the lad had set fire to the straw and then ran into the pigsty to escape from the smoke. No doubt he was suffocated and the raging fire completed the tragedy. I heard the details from my mother in the evening for I was at school during the fire and when I arrived home a man was stationed at the yard gate to forbid admittance to any curious sightseers.

Shoemaker was never the same after the death of his son but although I was only a schoolboy and he was well past middle age, he seemed always ready to have a chat with me. We had a common hobby, the collecting of old coins. He had a cocoa tin full of them and I had a score or two. I well remember a penny he had, I think it was George IV of an oval shape and in mint condition. I have never seen one like it since.

We had a reliable village carrier, Mr George Young. Three times a week Mr Young made the journey to town and back, twelve miles each way. No protection from the weather in his vehicle, a roomy wagonette. On the forward journey there was a steep, long hill to surmount. If heavily loaded, the male passengers would be asked to get out and walk. When, in the course of time, Carrier handed over the business to his two grown up sons they soon acquired a new up-to-date two-horsed bus, the last word in village transportation. All the villagers felt a personal pride in the vehicle. No more exposure to the elements, even Squire couldn't travel in more comfort, neither could he enjoy the gossip which was passed around in the friendly atmosphere of 'our new bus'.

Till the novelty wore off we nippers used to be on the lookout for its return from town in the evenings, as if it were some royal equipage. There were several seats on top near the driver but the main space there would be loaded with merchandise, for Carrier was always entrusted with many commissions from tradesmen who couldn't spare the time to go themselves. In the years when I was a pageboy our lady always hired this bus to take the indoor staff – each could invite a friend – for a trip to the seaside in the summer and again in the winter to town to see the pantomime.

Our village could also boast of a Drill Hall, headquarters of the Volunteers for miles around. Like all the other nippers in the village, I always liked to be present on drill nights in the summer, for then the men – a real imposing crowd – would be put through their exercises in the open space in front of the building.[20] I reckon many of us lads looked forward to the time when we would be big enough to carry a rifle, don a smart green uniform topped by an imposing helmet and swagger round the village.

One evening a big burly drover came up to the entrance gates and in a mocking tone echoed the officer's orders. Before he had done so many times, the officer gave the order 'Stand at ease', then he rushed across the few yards to the entrance and looking up into the drover's face (who was a much bigger man) he barked, 'Were you mocking me?' 'Oh, no, sir,' blurted the drover. 'If I was sure you were, I'd d★★★ well black your eyes for you!' The drover slunk off, accompanied by our laughter and jeers. The officer resumed his duties but I feel sure a number of us little rascals were disappointed that he didn't black the drover's eyes.

There were plenty of drovers about in those days and it was a very common occurrence for big herds of cattle and sheep to pass through the village en route to or from the big Bristol market. Very exhausted many of the poor animals were and the way in which those brutish drovers belaboured any which lagged behind was heartbreaking for any decent person to see. Garden gates had to be kept shut and fences in good order in our neighbourhood, or unwelcome visitors were pretty sure to damage or even destroy the crops.

In spring there would be many 'tater' carts on the road. These came chiefly from the Cheddar district. Going forward to Bristol Market they would be heavily loaded with baskets of early potatoes, returning with just a pile of empties every evening. Light one-horsed carts, always hurrying in the mornings but returning home in a much more leisurely manner, oftentimes the driver swaying about on his seat, apparently much more 'loaded up' than his vehicle!

Rural life

Some underlying themes recur throughout all the sections of Alfred's memoir. These include nostalgia for the rural way of life of his childhood memory, an affinity with the Somerset countryside and a countryman's love of animals (although, as will shortly be revealed, young Alfred and his friends had a pretty cavalier attitude towards the preservation of the local birdlife).

The 'coombe' to which Alfred refers on several occasions here is certainly Burrington Combe, a dramatic, steep-sided, rocky gorge within a couple of miles of Alfred's childhood home. Alfred recalls a quiet, lonely place where 'just a horse and cart occasionally on the road, or a gipsy van or two sheltered up in a side lane would be about all the traffic to be seen'.

Burrington Combe is now a popular attraction to walkers, climbers and cavers, and is protected as a Site of Special Scientific Interest. Since Alfred's day, one of Burrington Combe's caves, Aveline's Hole, has been discovered to contain a 10,000-year-old Mesolithic cemetery, the oldest-known cemetery in Britain and a site of international archeological importance. Other Mendip caves have rather less well-substantiated folkloric associations, a couple of which Alfred describes.

My elder brother was now pupil-teacher and always poring over his books, so all the odd jobs, indoors and out, fell to my lot.[21] Father owned a small flock of sheep and part of the year I had to drive them out to the common early in the morning and fetch them back home in the evening. Then for a long period they would be grazing up on the hills and I would have to go miles to find them to see they were alright, none on their backs and unable to get up – for when one got in that position it couldn't right itself but with my puny strength and its own struggles the job could be done. I had also to look out for lame ones or any affected by maggots – jobs too much for me to contend with but I had to report any such cases for the necessary treatment.

It was I who had to drive the flock to a neighbouring farm, where the lambs were treated and had their tails cut off. The operator would hold the poor little lamb between his legs, feel for a nick near the thick end of the tail. There was an upward pull of the knife and that tail would never wag again. I was offered the severed tails but I didn't accept although I was told that when skinned and fried, a good fat tail was very nice.

In those days when I was often sent up on the hills to locate father's sheep and see that they were in no trouble, one would seldom meet up with a single human being. On a fine summer day there might be a wagonette family party of picnickers down in the coombe, boiling water over a fire of sticks to make the always welcome cup o' tea. Best crystal clear water was always obtainable direct from a spring about fifty yards from the road or it could be dipped up from the overflow which ran for some little distance close to the side of the road, then disappeared into the ground to flow out in increased volume miles away.

Many acres of the hills would be covered in bracken, many more with short sweet grass – but what attracted visitors and sent some of them into raptures was the great expanse of purple heather which they would gather in big bunches. Generally a few minutes' search would be rewarded by a handful of the lucky white. It was a grand sight when in full bloom and when only a small boy I would gaze with admiration approaching awe as its beauty.

When the blackcurrants were ripening in the cottage gardens, then we all knew it was time to gather the 'worts' (whortleberries).[22] They grew only in certain places, all well known to the local people and visitors might wander about for hours on the hills and not see a berry. Sometimes in those far-off days they would fetch a shilling a quart. Every shilling was badly wanted by the labouring classes, so that women living near, helped by their children, would be after them early and late. Being such small berries it took an hour or two to pick a quart and if a previous picker had lately been over the patch one would be lucky to get a pint.

In late summer, many men living near would put in as much time as they could cutting bracken, which when dried was used for bedding for animals, chiefly for the cottagers' pigs. When dried and used for this purpose it was never called bracken but 'fern' or 'vearn'. After a man had cut as much as he required it might be left for weeks to dry before he fetched it away but I never heard of a man making off with a neighbour's cut of fern.

What was harvested in this way was only a small portion of what was left standing to ripen and wither as the winter approached. After a spell of dry weather in late autumn, one fine evening the hills would be one blaze of fire visible for miles around, the fern having been deliberately fired to clear the ground and allow the new growth of bracken to grow up unhindered in the spring.

On the outskirts of the hills were a number of 'hill gardens' so called – but there was little garden about them in my time, they were nearly all down to grass. My father claimed only one but he pointed out to me another one, much larger with the ruin of a stone house standing on it, which he said was once occupied by an ancestor of ours. He told me that it was the custom in the old days that if a man 'tined' or hedged in a small portion of the hill then, by paying a shilling a year fee to the Lord of the Manor, he could not be ousted from possession.

Father, being unable to carry out the condition of personally tending to this bit of property when he went to live in another village, allowed a neighbour to make use of it. A little later, on meeting the Lord of the Manor, he was told, 'As you are not making use of the garden it is now my property.' Father replied, 'Yes, I know.' In this informal way we lost the last bit of our ancestral holding. I often wonder what it is like now for it had about a fifty yard frontage on to a minor hard road and was consequently much easier of access than most of the other plots. About a half acre in extent, it was just a nice little building site.[23]

On the hillside near the village were many shallow pits locally known as 'gruff holes'[24] made by cottagers living near in the old days when they were seeking for calamine, a mineral only found in restricted areas. The gruff holes were only to be seen on a few parts of the hill on our side of the country. We had an old pick, for use in breaking coal which father said was used by his grandfather when he did a bit of this shallow mining.

There were several caves near the coombe. One had a large entrance hut but one had to get down on all fours to enter the others. I went in one of the latter one afternoon in company of two men visitors who were equipped with a big ball of twine and numerous candles. We were creeping and climbing about in there for about two hours and I was very glad to get out into daylight again for a false step or a slip in many places would have meant a broken limb or even loss of life.

There was a very deep hole in the rocks on the side of the coombe that was a great attraction to us schoolboys for if a big stone was tossed into it there would arise a series of bumps as if it was descending a long flight of stairs, then a final louder bang as if it had banged into a good solid oak door behind which it was rumoured the devil lived. My father told me that when he was a young man, a villager who had been indulging a bit too freely, determined to go down this hole to visit His Satanic Majesty. He got into difficulties and later his body was recovered. The hole is called by his name to this day.

At a certain spot near the entrance to the coombe, by climbing up the steep cliff side for about forty feet, one could reach 'Sweet Well' and always obtain a cool refreshing drink. I don't think any adults did so but active lads wouldn't miss the chance. Visitors would never find it unless directed by a native, for the water just trickled out of a cleft in the rock filling a small depression holding about a couple of quarts, then disappeared into the rock again, leaving no trace to advertise its existence. There was a lime kiln in working order quite close and years ago that mass of rock was quarried away and Sweet Well went with it.

Larks and blackcaps were numerous and I found many a cosy little lark's nest tucked away among the heather. Bird life was held in little regard when I was a boy. I well remember meeting up with an old chap one day when I was out with my catapult and about to aim at a chaffinch. 'Ah, kill all them finches,' said he, 'for they do eat up all the fruit buds and I do tear out any of their nests as I do come across.' Even as a boy I knew how the tits would spoil the peas. If they did not empty the pods from which they had abstracted one pea, the hole would permit the rain to enter and in a day or two the remaining peas would be mouldy.

Blackbirds and thrushes were just persistent gluttons for almost any kind of fruit. Netting or any other kind of protection was seldom seen in a cottage garden. It was too expensive. Parents generally encouraged their sons to scare

Two local girls pose for the photographer in Burrington Combe. (Post 1890, Stan Croker Collection)

off – or preferably to kill – these robbers and I must confess that I 'toppled over' a good many. But I was no nest robber as so many boys were.

There were two kinds of slings for hurling stones in common use. One was only a two foot length of a stout stick, split at the top. A stone was wedged in the split and by a whirl and a jerk could be thrown out with considerable force. The most favoured sling was made up of a piece of leather and two lengths of string, one piece about six inches shorter than the other. These were fastened to the leather patch in which a stone was placed. The sling was whirled round above the thrower's head and at the right split second the short piece of string was released and the stone sped to its target. It was really surprising how accurate and far a boy would hurl a stone after he had put in a year or so practising. I had little to do with slings, always favoured the catapult.

'Squailing' was a bird hunting game that didn't appeal to me. Several lads would fill their pockets and left hands with stones, always keeping a single one for first throw in the right hand. One or more boys would go along each side of a hedge till a bird was seen, then a fusillade of stones from each side of the hedge prevented the bird from breaking out and often it would be so frightened and confused that it was easily killed.

The one little bird that is generally respected, even by the most cruel boys, is the robin. I never knew of a boy killing one with deliberation but I had the misfortune to kill one by accident. I had come through the wood, catapult in hand, just potting at anything and hitting nothing, then, to get rid of the loaded stone, I pulled at a flying bird some dozen yards away and never expected to hit it. Going close up I saw it was a robin, stone dead. I was quite upset over this and never used my catapult in such a haphazard way afterwards.

There were several kinds of homemade traps in use. Sieve, wicker and brick all caught birds alive. Sparrows and blackbirds were often caught, cooked and eaten. I never tasted any but one of my mates assured me that sparrow pie or a toasted blackbird was delicious. Horsehair nooses, fish-hooks and steel traps were used for bigger birds. Wire nooses or steel gins for rabbits. Gamekeepers or 'bobbies' were very keen on catching poachers yet in most villages there was nearly sure to be a man or two could bring along a rabbit any time you asked him and often a bit of game too – no questions asked or answered as to where it came from.

On several occasions one winter I went out after dark, sparrow netting, in company with three grown men who owned a big long net. The net was stretched between two poles and held over the ivy-clad tree or under the eaves of thatched houses by two men while the third tickled the ivy or thatch with a slender pole to scare out the sheltering birds. I carried a bull's-eye lantern to enable them to see when they had a good catch. Then the net would be lowered and the trapped sparrows transferred to a woman's long stocking. Another stocking was reserved for any singing birds that were caught. They would be disposed of as cage birds. The sparrows were in demand for shooting matches. The owner of the net knew just where to place them but the cash receipts were very poor and I, as an apprentice, got nothing, so I soon tired of that game.

Many boys had a tame jackdaw but they seldom lived more than a year. I had one for months but as nesting time came around again he began taking an occasional 'day off' so I decided to clip his wings. I was silly enough to clip both and had the mortification of seeing 'Jack' after a struggle, rise up in the air and fly slowly off, never to return. Of course, if I'd clipped only the one wing, he couldn't have kept on an even keel and wouldn't have got far.

A widow living about a half mile from our school owned a jackdaw and this scoundrel of a bird would fly down among the infant children as they were near school and peck at their little naked legs, causing a lot of squeaking and some tears. Though many kicks and blows were aimed at the rascal he was so nimble that he never suffered any damage and after a few minutes diversion, would fly off chuckling as if he had thoroughly enjoyed the commotion he had created. But little pecked legs couldn't be borne in silence and later through complaints from parents, the owner curtailed her bird's liberty.

I have found a great many of our wild birds' nests but never but one of the gold crested wren and that was tied up so neatly on the underside of a fir branch about six feet from the ground.[25] Edward stood unsteadily on my shoulders to reach it and had the misfortune to break an egg or two in the nest when trying to get one out for our collection – tiny eggs, about the size of a small green pea. We both regretted damaging the nest for, as was to be expected, the birds forsook it.

'Squire'

As his father's employer and landlord, and the most important member of the Langford community, 'Squire' is an absolutely central figure in Alfred's childhood recollections. Squire was Evan Henry Llewellyn (1847–1914).

Llewellyn was born at Clydach, near Swansea. His father Llewellyn Llewellyn was a local industrialist who owned the Ynyspenllwch tinplate works. After his father's death in 1859, Evan's family lived in a substantial village house in rural Oxfordshire and young Evan may have attended Rugby School (his older brother is recorded as a pupil at Rugby in 1861). In other words, the Llewellyn family seems to have followed a well-worn nineteenth-century path making, over the course of a couple of generations, the transition from successful business people to landed gentry. Evan gave his occupation at the 1871 census as 'Landowner' and at the 1881 census as 'Justice of the Peace'.

Evan Henry Llewellyn MP,
from an engraving made in
the 1880s. (David Wilkins'
collection)

MR. E. H. LLEWELLYN—NORTH SOMERSET

In 1868, Evan had married 21-year-old Mary Blanche Somers (1847–1906).
Mary was born and raised at Mendip Lodge in Upper Langford. Presumably
it was his marriage to Mary that brought Evan to live in Somerset. Evan and
Mary had five sons and two daughters, born between 1870 and 1881. Mary's
father, Thomas Somers, was a barrister by profession but he does not appear
to have practised law during Mary's childhood.[26] Instead he was managing the
400-acre estate he had inherited from his father, which included, at least for a
while, a lead-mining and smelting operation.[27]

The position of Justice of the Peace that Evan was to hold for much of
his adult life was an important and powerful one. In addition to carrying
out the kinds of judicial functions associated with a present-day magistrate,
Justices of the Peace at this time also held senior responsibility for the
regulation and administration of rural counties such as Somerset (elected
county councils were not introduced until 1888). Evan was also deputy
lieutenant of Somerset.

In 1885 Evan was elected as Conservative MP for the Somerset Northern division. He lost the seat at the 1892 election but was elected again in 1895 and served until 1906 when he retired from politics. At some point during his political career he became a lieutenant colonel in the Somersetshire Light Infantry. This appears perhaps to have been an honorary commission, but at some point around that time onwards he adopted the military title and was generally known as Colonel Evan Llewellyn.

Interestingly, given subsequent events in Alfred's own story, Evan later became a director of the GWR. He died in 1914 at the home of his daughter, Mercy, in Clyst St George, Devon.[28] His body was returned to Burrington for burial in a ceremony on board a specially timetabled GWR train.[29]

Alfred portrays Evan as widely liked and respected by the local community, including by Alfred and his family (although he could also be short-ish of temper, as will later be seen). Certainly Evan did not neglect his responsibilities to his staff and tenants or to the wider village community. At this time, the old idea of *noblesse oblige* – that those who enjoyed the benefits of privilege had an inherent duty to perform acts of generosity and kindness towards those who did not – was still ingrained into country life. 'Squire' Llewellyn appears to have taken seriously his obligations in this respect.

Squire gave his staff an early evening supper near Christmas Day after which all who cared to could fetch their children along to see the most gaily decorated Christmas tree, on which there would be a present for everyone. I had a good-sized bottle of scent one time. I didn't want it and started looking round for a particular little lady friend to make her a present of it when, on passing through a doorway, I was pushed against a post. The bottle, in my coat pocket, was broken and the liquid soaked through and ran all down my leg. Everyone I came near that evening took a second sniff at me.

Squire also built a 'Reading Room' for the villagers long before any of the other villages near could boast of such a building. He provided it with many books, a bagatelle table and other games. A Committee was appointed and one of them was supposed to be in attendance every evening to keep order. The caretaker lived in an adjoining cottage and through a small door provided in the wall, he would pass tea, coffee or cocoa at a penny a time and biscuits at the same price.

Edward and I went there occasionally for a month or two, but by then the Committee had failed in their duty and seldom attended. The rougher lot of youths had got out of control, rowdyism and bad language prevailed, so that all decent-minded lads kept away. Squire's generosity was wasted for the room became deserted.

Every summer Squire gave a gigantic tea-party for all the children in the parish and any living outside if they attended our school. To provide music, a band of sailor lads from the 'Formidable' training ship was in attendance and a real smart lot they were with their gleaming brass instruments and all dressed in their best uniforms.[30] The squire's two teenage daughters, assisted by friends, used to see to the needs of us nippers at teatime and made fine fun of it, encouraging us to eat and drink to the very limit of our capacity. Then they would bunch up and wrangle as to who had the champion glutton in her care.

Squire also sent wagons to the workhouse to fetch all the inmates who were in good enough health to come to the garden party. They arrived for midday lunch and left again soon after tea for it was about a six mile journey for them. The men all wore smocks and the women print dresses, shawls and poke bonnets. The men were given tobacco and the women packets of sweets and I guess it was a red letter day for them.

Although not named, the workhouse from which the inmates were invited to Evan Llewellyn's garden party seems certain to have been the one at Axbridge.[31] Lower Langford and Burrington fell within the Axbridge Poor Law Union (the administrative district that defined the catchment area for a particular workhouse). The work of Poor Law Unions was managed by a group of Poor Law Guardians, who were elected by local property owners. Any Justice of the Peace resident in a Poor Law Union automatically became a Poor Law Guardian. Not only was Evan therefore among the guardians for the Axbridge Union he was, at least for a time in the mid 1880s, the chairman of the Board of Guardians.[32] He would therefore have felt a particular responsibility towards the inmates. The workhouse at Axbridge was built in 1834 and provided places for up to 250 destitute residents from a population of around 30,000 people in the villages of the western Mendips. The workhouse building still stands.

It seems unlikely that all (or even, most of) the 250 Axbridge inmates could have been transported over to Langford Court for Squire's garden party so presumably the privilege was limited to those who had, in better days, been resident in Upper and Lower Langford and the surrounding villages. What a bitter-sweet experience it must have been for them. On the one hand the pleasure of a day out and the joy of seeing relatives and old friends; on the other, the humiliation of returning to their home area as workhouse inmates and the sad realisation that they must climb onto the wagon and be taken back to Axbridge at the end of the day.

I saw the squire only twice after I reached man's estate. Once when I was at a railway station of a populous village he came there to address a political meeting. He arrived by train. There was a big crowd to meet him including all the 'big shots' for several miles around, for election fever was rampant. He was M.P. for the Division and standing for re-election. I was collecting the tickets and as he came up, he looked me in the face and said 'Why, it's young Plumley. How are you?' I feel sure my reputation with the villagers went up 100% because of that greeting but I can't think how he recognised me for it must have been five years or so since we met and I'd grown from a weedy lad into a stout young fellow.

Another twenty years passed and I took my son, a lad of fourteen, to ask Squire to use his influence to get the lad a start on the railway clerical staff. The dear gentleman, now elderly and infirm, received us most kindly. He did not rise from his big easy chair but beckoned my son to him. He put his arm round his shoulders and studied his face, then said 'He's one of the old stock. I will do all I can for him.' He died a short time afterwards and although he left five sons and two daughters, there is now no-one living in the locality bearing the old family name.

Squire and Freddy part company

Sometime around 1884, an incident occurred which threatened to undermine the entire structure of the Plumley family's life in Lower Langford. As it turned out, the problem had a speedy and happy resolution – albeit one that involved a major change in the family's living circumstances. It was this change that laid the foundations for the next big step in Alfred's life.

When I was about ten years of age, what we thought at the time was a big misfortune happened to father. Squire bought – in his opinion – a very fine trap horse. But father and his old friend the blacksmith had a different idea of the animal. I was present one day when, after shoeing him, the smith said 'Ee ain't firm on his legs Freddy, ee'll let somebody down one day.' I'm sure father would most willingly have refuted his friend's words if he had not been of the same opinion himself, for he was always proud and considerate of any animal in his charge and especially so of a horse. He had piles of books concerning the horse which he must have bought in his youth. Those books, the Bible and a weekly newspaper comprised all the reading matter he had, to my knowledge, studied. I feel sure he was very disappointed that none of his sons showed any interest in his 'horse books'. They must have cost him many of his hard-earned shillings.

Anyhow, from the large number and variety of horses that the smith handled and my father's care of the squire's, coupled with his book knowledge, I reckon they could size up a horse as well as most men.

It was only a week or so after Smith had declared his opinion of Squire's latest addition to his stud that his words came true. Squire and father had been off in the trap behind this horse on some business miles away when, on returning, Squire decided to pay a visit to a neighbour and instructed father to drive on as he would walk home later. A few minutes later as father was leisurely driving home, down went the horse! 'Broke his knees!' was the verdict. No other damage but that was enough – he'd be no good as a showy trap horse again.

Squire was furious, accused father of carelessness and bullied father so much that father took the drastic step of giving Squire notice to leave his service after fifteen years in his employ, during which he had given every satisfaction. Naturally, mother was very upset. Good situations were hard to get and with us youngsters to feed and clothe, any small amount of savings they had managed to put by would soon disappear now no weekly wage could be expected.

The first day he was free, father walked off to a parsonage about eight miles away where he heard a coachman was wanted. He returned late in the evening, tired out and in no good spirits. It appeared it was a very poor place and he'd be more of an odd-job man than a coachman, so he had come to no decision as to accepting the post.

As matters turned out, it was a good thing he did not bind himself. Next day he had a note from Squire's wife's mother, Elizabeth Somers, who lived with her son at Mendip Lodge, a fine mansion a few miles away. Father was to come and see her. Hoping for the best, off he went. The old lady told him she had decided to buy a pair of carriage horses of her own (hitherto she had depended upon those belonging to her son) and she would need her own coachman. Would father enter her service? I can imagine father's relief – and what a pleasure it was to him to bring home the comforting news to mother and us youngsters. Father would get his usual wage and would be allotted a good sound thatched cottage rent-free.

Now I believe all this was engineered by the squire's wife, Mrs Mary Llewellyn. She was a real practising Christian lady and revered by everyone who knew her. She had seen father soon after the break between him and Squire and had begged him to do nothing in a hurry, as she felt sure there might be a reconciliation. Failing to do this and no doubt being aware of her mother's wish to have horses of her own, she had persuaded her to send for father and engage him as coachman.

The cottage destined to be our future home for some years was situated in a beautiful bit of country. Quarter of a mile away was 'Springhead', so called because a crystal clear spring of water issued up there and spread out in a wide shallow stream to flow within a few yards of our cottage. We all obtained any necessary water from this source. We lads also used to catch loggerheads and occasional loach, and fairly often a beautiful speckled trout, mostly small ones but sometimes they'd be big enough for the frying-pan.

Father sold off what pigs he had for there was no sty attached to our new home but we took a good number of poultry. Just then the sheep were up on the hills but were also sold before winter set in and I'm sure father benefited in health by having so much less to do. He'd been trying to do two men's work and it didn't pay. Mother and us nippers were relieved of so many odd jobs that had been expected of us. However, mother soon had another task on her hands, for two elderly ladies living next door asked for her help a good deal and they got it until one died and the other went to relations. Then later she had father's mother, a bedridden old lady, to care for. Very little leisure had my mother in all her life, yet always cheerful and on the spot when wanted for any emergency.

There was a coachman – such a fat fellow – and a groom already at the stables, father making a third. They agreed well together and I know we were all much happier. The estate was a large one. The owner was spoken of by his tenants as the 'Guv'nor' or 'Squire' so that I allude to him henceforward as another 'Squire'. There was sure to be one living in a big house on the outskirts of most country villages.

A month or so after father had left his old employer under such unpleasant circumstances, they met up near the Court. Squire Llewellyn took father in. I don't know what actually passed between them but father came home with a beaming face. All bad feeling was forgotten. Squire had given father a money present and his photograph. I have the photo now. He was a fine man, perhaps a bit hasty but it is presumptuous of me to size up such an influential, clever gentleman.

Springhead, Upper Langford. The site of a natural spring, just ¼ mile from the Plumley family's new home on the Mendip Lodge Estate. (Post 1890, Stan Croker Collection)

Family and Circumstances, 1886

Alfred

Alfred Plumley leaves school at the end of June 1886, a week short of his twelfth birthday. He goes immediately to work as a pageboy at Mendip Lodge near Burrington, where his father now works as a coachman.

The phrase 'pageboy' calls to mind a kind of courtly personal attendant but the reality of the job by the nineteenth century was quite different. The household 'page' of this period was essentially an apprentice footman. He was usually a local lad, thought capable of being trained as a house-servant and of progressing up the hierarchy of domestic staff. He might still have to wear livery on formal occasions (as Alfred did) but the majority of his work was as an odd-job boy. He would run errands, take messages and generally fetch and carry for members of his employing family. He might also be expected – as was the case for Alfred – to act as a spare pair of hands for the specialist staff, both indoor and outdoor, from the gamekeeper and groom to the butler and cook. As can easily be imagined, the position of a small boy employed in this type of role was firmly at the bottom of the household pecking order.

Freddy Plumley and the Plumley family

Freddy had a falling out with his previous employer, 'Squire' Evan Llewellyn of Langford Court, and felt obliged to resign as Squire's coachman after fifteen years' service. Freddy's rift with Squire was quickly repaired but not before Freddy had found new employment at nearby Mendip Lodge, where he is one of two coachmen in post. It is not clear exactly when Freddy and Squire parted company but it seems to have been later in Alfred's schooldays, perhaps when Alfred was aged 10 or 11 in 1884 or 1885. The Plumley family has now moved to a cottage belonging to the Mendip Lodge estate where they are happily settled. The move has had a particular benefit for Mary, who has been freed from the restrictions of her duties as gatekeeper at Langford Court. Edward Plumley, Alfred's elder brother, now works as a pupil-teacher at Burrington Primary School (see note 22 of chapter 2).

Mendip Lodge

Mendip Lodge was a house of unusual and rather exotic appearance built in the late eighteenth century. The history of the house and Alfred's description of it are given in the following chapter. Mendip Lodge was demolished in the 1950s.

The Somers family

The senior occupant of Mendip Lodge while Alfred works there is Elizabeth Somers, aged 65. Elizabeth is the widow of Thomas Somers and mother of Mary Llewellyn, wife of Freddy Plumley's former employer Evan Llewellyn. Freddy is employed as Elizabeth's personal coachman.

Also resident at Mendip Lodge are Elizabeth's son, Benjamin Somers, aged 35, and his wife Agnes. In this forthcoming part of Alfred's story, it is now Benjamin to whom Alfred now refers as 'Squire', rather than his father's former employer, Evan Henry Llewellyn. Benjamin is a barrister but, like his father before him, is not practising. During the course of the story, the household is joined by Rose Stewart, sister of Benjamin Somers and Mary Llewellyn. Rose had the misfortune to be widowed four times during her life. In 1886, she is in her second period of widowhood, her second husband, a clergyman, having died in 1883. It is Rose who exhibits the fickle attitude to dog ownership of which Alfred so disapproves.

2

ALFRED PLUMLEY

SERVANT

Alfred goes to work

One fine morning at school there was a buzz of excitement, for every boy
was given a numbered ticket and a pin with which to attach it to his coat. We
knew from previous experience that this meant it was 'Examination Day'.

The teachers were smartened up and even Schoolmaster had a wintry
kind of smile on his face but he looked half dressed, for he wasn't carrying
his dreaded stick. His year's work was about to be tested and he may have
felt a trifle nervy himself for a bad report on progress might cost him his job.
A week or so later I knew I had passed the 5th Standard and would soon be
leaving school.[1]

Before I was released from school my father took me for an interview
at Mendip Lodge, with Squire[2] who required a page boy. I was engaged at
once – £3 a year and 'all found'.[3] Within a few days however, the school
authorities notified my parents that, as I was not yet twelve years of age, I
must return to school.

My brother, who was now a paid pupil teacher, fairly gloated over my
summons to return, as if he had engineered the affair all on his own but
somehow Schoolmaster was squared. I had orders to show up at school to
get a tick on the register then, at a nod from Schoolmaster, I was free for the
day. It was only the matter of a week or so to my twelfth birthday, then it was
a final goodbye to school life.

'A spacious mansion ... 500 acres with extensive rights'

Mendip Lodge was a strikingly unusual building with an elegant, covered verandah running the full width of the front elevation. It was commissioned in the late eighteenth century by the wealthy writer, traveller and socialite Rev. Dr Thomas Sedgwick Whalley. Whalley lived in Bath, where he owned the centre house in the Royal Crescent and was a well-known figure in the social life of the city.[4] He built Mendip Lodge primarily as a summer retreat. The lodge was situated on the edge of a high, steep hillside above the villages of Burrington and Upper Langford and had uninterrupted views toward the Severn Estuary.

At Rev. Whalley's death in 1828, Mendip Lodge was inherited by his nephew James Wickham. The house subsequently passed to Wickham's daughter, Mary, who died in 1840. It was sold by her widower, Major William Fawcett, in 1845 to the Somers family. An advertisement for the sale described Mendip Lodge as:

> a spacious mansion, with extensive plantations, gardens, grounds, stables, offices, valuable enclosures of arable and pasture land, a rabbit warren and sheep walk, containing together 500 acres with extensive rights on a neighbouring common. From the extraordinary beauty of the surrounding country, the property is particularly eligible as a residence for a nobleman or man of fortune ... The mansion is surrounded by healthy plantations in which are walks and carriage drives on the green sward and a charming turf terrace of half a mile leading to Burrington Church ... There are 11 bedrooms besides dressing rooms, a dining room 33 feet by 21, a suite of drawing rooms of moderate dimensions and the usual attached and detached domestic offices.[5]

Alfred describes Mendip Lodge himself in his memoir.

The house was situated on high ground and surrounded by trees. The carriage drive leading to it was a mile long. Laurels, laurustinus and many shrubs I cannot name bordered the drive. High above them towered acacia and lime

Mendip Lodge, the grand home of the Somers family, where both Alfred and his father worked – Alfred as a pageboy and Freddy as a coachman. (Post 1890, Stan Croker Collection)

trees. All wheeled traffic had to come up this zigzag drive to reach the house but practically all persons on foot reached it by a much shorter but very steep footpath. What a beautiful place it was in the summer! A verandah ran along the whole length of the front and generally there would be several peafowl present, the cock-birds always ready to display their magnificent fan shaped tails to one and all. They were really fine birds.

The house was quite a show–place inside and out. All the best rooms were on the first floor as looked at from the front but owing to the sloping ground many were really the ground floor on the other side. There were the 'Painted Rooms', a long series of rooms with very large mirrors at each end. These were inclined to give one the impression that it was possible to walk on indefinitely but brass rods were fitted across them about waist high to prevent accidents. The walls were adorned by beautifully painted country scenery and were the chief attraction to all visitors. Big French windows allowed one to walk out on the upper floor of the verandah from which there was a grand view over the country for miles.

There was a large dining-room, on the walls of which and in the passage leading to it, hung portraits of Squire's ancestors. At the extreme end of this room there was a small door rarely noticed by anyone and this led to what the maid-servants called the 'Haunted Room'. I saw the butler coming out through the door one day and this was the only occasion I know of anyone ever visiting it. I know the maids shunned that part and the rumour was that a mad relative of a former owner had been confined and died there. A strongly barred window hardly noticeable from outside admitted light.

Squire's mother, Mrs Elizabeth Somers, claimed a large bow-windowed room on the ground floor at one end of the building and round this window were many halves of what had originally been big round reddish stones but they had been broken open to expose the sparkling quartz contents. I asked one of the old gardeners what the stones were called and he said they were 'Mendip diamonds'. I was always on the lookout for one of these round

Mendip Lodge seen from road level. (Stan Croker Collection (original photograph c.1935 by George Love Dafnis))

stones about the size of a football – but never found one. Must have been rare for I never knew of a cottager to possess one.

There were several flower beds in the lawn outside the bay window and the old lady would always have these planted, principally with heliotrope ('cherry pie' to us country folk) and on a fine summer day the fragrance of this plant just filled the air.

Red squirrels were numerous in the woods, so much so at one time Squire told the keeper to shoot some of them as he considered they were doing much damage to the young trees he had planted. Pheasants were to be met with nearly everywhere most of the year but they were nearly all birds that had been hatched out by the common domestic hen and not given their liberty till they were fully fledged, then later in the year they provided sport for the shooting parties.

Every Sunday morning the indoor staff walked to Burrington Church for service going by a wide path known as the 'Golden Walk'. For about a half mile this path was overhung with laburnum trees and when these trees were in bloom nobody could deny but that it was most aptly named, just one long bower of gold. There were several seats at intervals and near the end a big roomy summerhouse.

At the entrance gates to the house were two small round thatched houses, one used as a living room and the other as a bedroom by the lodge-keeper and his wife, a childless couple who had to cross the drive every night to reach their bed. The 'Pepper Pots' was the name by which these quaint little houses were known.

The tenant of the Pepper Pots was an elderly, bent man and was always addressed as 'Dangee' by his fellow employees and by most of the other folk in the neighbourhood. The old chap acquired this name through his habit of always saying 'dang 'ee' to any tool he was using or to any person that failed to please him – his invariable way of expressing his displeasure. He had worked on the estate for many years and in my time was too frail and crippled by rheumatism to do any hard work. About his only duty was to keep the long carriage drive clear of fallen leaves, cleaning out the gutters and trimming the bushes on the sides. You could always find Dangee on some part of the drive, or resting up in the summer house, situated about half way.

The 'Pepper Pots' – the twin gatehouses to Mendip Lodge and the home of 'Dangee' and his wife. Mendip Lodge itself is just visible halfway up the hillside. (Post 1890, Stan Croker Collection)

Getting the hang of the job

At first I was employed on any odd job but the butler gradually instructed me in permanent duties, such as opening the front door to visitors, delivering cards and notes on a salver, and announcing callers – first ascertaining if the person enquired for was 'at home'.

This 'at home' business puzzled me, for I'd been brought up to be truthful and it didn't seem right to say 'not at home' when it was told me by the very person enquired for. Anyhow, I must have shown promise, for the tailor arrived and I was measured up for a suit of livery in dark green, a dark pair of trousers and two washable coats for morning wear. A top coat with silver-plated crested buttons, top hat, thin leather gloves and a pair of patent leather shoes completed the outfit.

Now that I was equipped as one of the staff, I had to attend church service every Sunday morning in my best silver buttoned livery and top hat, wearing or carrying my gloves. Butler, three or four maids and a groom made up our usual party and we always occupied two pews reserved for us. Squire generally attended the services and read the lessons. My special school chum warned me that several of the rowdiest lads meant to fetch my 'topper' off as soon as I left the churchyard. I noticed them waiting about for this purpose but I foiled them by keeping close to the butler's side. They couldn't attempt such an outrage under his eye.

I was soon aware there was no leisure time for me. At 7.00 a.m. I was off to the farm to get a four gallon can of milk. When I arrived with the milk the girls were usually enjoying their first cup of tea and, of course, there was one for me. Then it was cleaning boots till eight when I was off to the post office, two miles away, with a big private letter bag in which Postmaster put all household letters and locked the bag before handing it over to me. This had to be in Squire's hands before 9 o'clock.

The maids were often asking me to keep their letters out of the bag for, of course, they had sweethearts and didn't want Squire to know every time they received a letter. Sometimes Postmaster would, at my request, hand over letters for Miss So-and-So and sometimes he would not – or could not be bothered – for there would be two postmen and another 'private bag' man receiving theirs and he and his wife, who helped him, very seldom got into 'top gear'. However, I did all I could to oblige the girls in this respect and we were the best of friends.

A big bell hung in a brick archway on top of the house. If I was a bit late with the mailbag with the morning's post, the butler was in the habit of clanging it a few times to hurry me up, for Squire got impatient if his letters were not in his hands on time – although, as the mailbags were brought from the junction eight miles away by an old uniformed postman in a high dogcart drawn by a steady old horse, punctuality could not always be relied upon, especially in winter.

After my delivery of the postbag I was always ready for breakfast which seldom varied; home-made bread, sweet as a nut, best farmhouse butter and a huge mug of tea. I never wished for anything better. Our housekeeper's bread was famous and I know she used to treat some of her best friends to a loaf pretty frequently. I earned my share of it, for I had to get the necessary wood to heat the oven from the woodhouse quarter of a mile away, first cutting it to the required length.

I was never short of a job, for Housekeeper and Lady's Maid always wanted something done and considered I was the one to do it. There were gold and silver pheasants and peafowl kept round the house and I had sole care of them. Near midday Butler claimed me and I was hustled into livery and having previously been shown how to lay table for lunch, I had now to wait at table. A few months later I was kept on to wait at late dinner, a duty I performed so well that Squire said I should have £6 a year instead of the £3 agreed upon. A visitor's lady's maid once gave me a real golden half sovereign, which she said her mistress had sent to me because I mimicked the butler so well! It was a pleasure to take the little gold coin home to mother and she was very amused to hear how I had come by it.

Fun and games below stairs

Like any workplace, 'downstairs' at Mendip Lodge was not immune to its staff relieving the tedium of the working day by some having a bit of fun at each other's expense. Alfred is by no means alone in still being able to recall these light-hearted moments later in life, when the day-to-day detail of the work itself has long faded from memory. It is particularly interesting to see that although Alfred has a full-time job and carries a number of responsibilities in the household, the butler and the maids often seem to perceive him as what he actually is – still just a small boy.

When Squire gave a big dinner party, Aaron Harris, a former butler was engaged for the evening.[6] He was a very pompous old chap but still active. He even did a postal round though unable to read or write. He knew the name of everyone living in the neighbourhood and as Postmaster gave him the letters singly he would keep them in rotation for delivery. If he got a bit muddled sometimes, you were allowed to pick your own and it worked out alright.

One evening after a dinner party we had cleared the table, washed up the silver and glass, and had a short interval before taking in the coffee. Aaron was not used to such late hours and was fast asleep in an easy chair, snoring away and nodding his head very sedately. Sam, the footman, said to me, 'Let's have a bit of fun with old Aaron. Get a tablespoon and put a bit of live coal in it.' I did this and Sam got a tin of cayenne pepper from a cupboard and liberally sprinkled the hot coal from it, causing penetrating fumes to arise.

Sam took the spoon from me and held it under Aaron's nose but the old chap gave a nod just then and went right down on the spoon. What a commotion! The spoon and contents went flying away, Aaron let out a yell and bounded from the chair, kicking it over and fetched up against the opposite wall. Before he got on his legs Sam and I were out of the room and a minute later we crowded in with the other servants to see what the row was about.

The butler was there now and Aaron was storming at him and demanding to see the squire to get justice. He couldn't say who were the culprits though and gradually the butler cooled him down for he wasn't really hurt except in his dignity. The servants' hall adjoined the pantry and the guests' coachmen were there – a lively lot – and they were so amused that they were all under suspicion whilst Sam and I, being amongst the last to arrive on the scene, were well in the clear.

Gentry in Victorian days liked to have fat coachmen in their service and our people must have considered the senior coachman a real prize for he was fat as they make 'em. Only about five feet seven inches in height but he was as near round in shape as a man could be – and strange to say, his wife was of a very similar build. They had no children and always showed quite a parental interest in me. To see the old chap climb up to the box seat of a carriage was really amusing. He'd hold to anything within reach, puff, grunt and jerk himself upwards, then having got into his seat, wouldn't leave it again till the return to the stables unless there should be a long interval, with refreshments, at some place of call. But he was no shirker of work and would bustle around, washing carriages, cleaning harness, and hiss away when grooming a horse as well as any man. He and my father got on well together.

I am afraid I played rather a scurvy trick on the old chap one evening but I must digress to say how it came about. One evening, when I was waiting at late dinner – I forget the exact number at table, about ten, I think – dessert was served and as I went to the mistress's side for some purpose, my foot touched something which gave out a sharp 'ting'. My lady jumped up

The stable yard at Mendip Lodge, domain of Freddy Plumley and senior coachman 'Bumble'. (Date unknown, Stan Croker Collection)

exclaiming 'I'm wet, I'm wet!' There was a look of amazement on the faces of the company at table, to be replaced by broad smiles as my lady, very red in the face, hurriedly left the room. She must have felt terribly embarrassed observing those smiles but I picked up her empty finger bowl from the floor and that explained the commotion. She had put that down by her chair for her wretched pet dog to drink from and I, on coming close, had kicked it over so that the water splashed all up her legs. Squire merely remarked, 'She should never have put it there.' I had no censure from anyone for actually causing the trouble but an order went out from somewhere that the dog was never to be allowed in the dining room at meal times again.

A few days after we had a big dinner party and the stable staff had to don their best livery and come in to assist. We all knew there was a fine salmon for dinner and 'Bumble' – that was the name bestowed on the senior coachman by us, his fellow employees – said, 'I don't want anything except a bit of that fish.'[7] Turning to me he said, 'Don't you whisk that off to the kitchen before I get a chance at it.'

The fish, what remained of it, came out of the dining room in due course and I came out just in time to see Bumble disappear through the Smoke Room door carrying a plate containing a good helping of his favourite delicacy. He couldn't stop to eat it then but returned to his duties. Then I caught sight of Annie, the head housemaid.[8] 'Hi, Nance,' said I, 'Would you like a nice bit of salmon?' 'Not half,' said she, so I told her Bumble had just hidden up a nice plateful in the Smoke Room. 'I'll see to it,' said Nance.

Dinner over, the gents settled to their wine and the ladies were in the drawing room. Several of us menials were in the pantry preparing to wash up the glass and silver when Bumble entered looking a picture of woe. Someone said, 'Had your bit of salmon?' 'No, I haven't,' he murmured. 'I put it under the couch in the Smoke Room and when I opened the door that brute of a dog rushed out and all my fish was gone. Annie must have shut the little beast in there.'

Smart girl, our Annie. No blame could be attached to her for she had orders to keep the dog out of the dining room. We had a laugh over it later and Nance assured me it was a delicious piece of salmon. I felt a bit sorry for old Bumble. He never recovered his good spirits that evening. But the ways of the transgressor are hard.

One day I saw what I thought was an unusually long feather from the tail of pheasant lying on some dead leaves on the ground. It was such a long one and barred so nicely that I stooped down to pick it up, then just as my fingers were closing on it, it moved forward! I jumped back for I never did like snakes. I could not find stick or stone near so shouted to the under-gardener who was tidying the path, a man generally known as 'Grim Death' or 'Grim' for short (I was so used to hearing him called by this name that I never enquired the reason). He ran along with a shovel and killed the snake before it could reach cover. He tied a bit of string round its neck and I took it to the house to terrify the younger maids with it. Afterwards, Butler measured it, just three feet two inches. Of course, only a harmless grass snake but I don't like snakes – and neither did the maids!

Being a hilly country there was plenty of sloping ground everywhere so that when a snowfall came it was every boy's ambition to have a little sled of his own, to experience the joy of a rush downhill. Our butler made me a real good stout sled but I had very little chance to use it. Just on a fair moonlight night, when I really ought to have been in bed, I might get an hour or so with it but no matter how early or late I got off duty, I had to deliver the milk about 7.00 a.m. Anyhow, if I couldn't use it, one of my mates had the loan of it.

The squire's family owned a smart roomy toboggan and well I knew it, for on fine afternoons, helped by a lad from the gardens, I was sent to drag this vehicle back to the top again after its downward rush full of giggling young ladies. Of course there would be an occasional spill that would cause a fine display of frills and flounces. We two lads would modestly look the other way but were bound to see the best of it because one never knew when it was coming. Anyhow, we all got a thrill out of it. After a spill or two the sport was always abandoned. I expect some snow penetrated to where it felt wet and unpleasant and it was 'home for a change'.

To see our butler so sedate and proper when on duty one would never think he could unbend so much as to make a sled for a lad but he was a real versatile character and would often entertain us as a conjuror, for he possessed quite a quantity of the stock required. Sometimes I had to be his helper. He would lie on the floor, arms outstretched, bring his feet up and I had to stand on his hands, lean on his feet and then he would throw me in a somersault to the end of the room. Again, I would be told 'stand firm' and he would grasp me below the knees, lift me high in the air and carry me around, I having to keep perfectly rigid during the tour.[9]

Squire owned a painting *The Blue Grotto* and one time when they – the family – were away for a change, Butler got this painting from the frame and copied it so faithfully that when he invited us, the indoor and several of the outdoor staff, to say which was the original, no one could tell.[10] They were as alike as the proverbial two peas. Our head gardener was a smart, well educated man but even he would not venture an opinion.

Most of the maidservants were fond of card games, and the groom and I were too. I was uncannily lucky, sometimes gaining several shillings in an evening's gamble. I used to be very amused at the little burst of temper the maids showed as I raked in their coppers. These little evening amusements only occurred when 'our folk' were gone out to a dinner party for, as they entertained a good deal, naturally they were invited back in return.

Once a year we were treated by our lady to a visit to the pantomime in Bristol. We saw very little of the city on these trips for the bus set us down in the Haymarket and we walked through Christmas Street up to the Prince's Theatre. We had no time to go about the town, we arrived just soon enough to reach the theatre in good time for the evening performance. What a wonderful sight the first pantomime seems to a youngster, and the Prince's Theatre was very famous for its fine shows.[11]

It was in a small tobacconist's shop near the theatre that I bought my first packet of cigarettes, being encouraged to do so by our head gardener's son who also purchased a packet. Tiny little geranium scented things they were. I didn't enjoy them and it was a long time before I entered a tobacconist's shop again. However, we puffed those tiny fags away to impress the girls and they were not strong enough to upset us.

My next visit to town was far from pleasant. It happened when our gentry were away visiting. Sam, the footman, proposed to me that we should go there one afternoon, returning by the last train in the evening. Just then, there

Mendip Lodge viewed from the rear gardens. (Date unknown, Stan Croker Collection)

was much talk of the American warship *Enterprise* being in Bristol dock and we meant to get a sight of her.[12]

We arrived in town all right and put in several hours sightseeing and then walked down the dock-side where we met up with a boatman and asked him as to the whereabouts of the *Enterprise*. 'She's berthed farther down the river,' said he, 'Row 'ee down to her for eighteen-pence?' We accepted his offer and off we went, till later the old chap ceased rowing and said, 'She must have gone out on the last tide, for she ain't here now.' Sam said, 'Then we'll go back.' But the old pirate replied, 'I shall want another shilling to take 'ee back.' When Sam demurred he contended that we had only engaged him to take us <u>to</u> the *Enterprise* and he thought we were going on board. Rubbish, of course, but as he showed no sign of starting back without being paid the shilling, he got it, for we were late as it was.

On our arrival back by train at the Junction, we found the last branch train had gone, so instead of a four mile walk from the branch station, we now had to do a ten mile walk from the Junction.[13] As neither of us was familiar with the road (for remember there were no bicycles then to enable one to take long rides and familiarise oneself with the countryside) this was a desperate situation. We had been on our legs all day but started off in pretty good spirits. After a hour's walk we came to a parting of the road and Sam insisted that we should take the turning to the left hand but my homing instinct told me very decidedly that he was wrong and, as neither of us would give way, we parted company.

I plodded timidly on, all on my own in the darkness. I could see just enough to keep on the road and that was all. Another half hour's trudging and I was getting really doubtful as to whether Sam had not known best, for I could not yet discern any familiar landmark. Then, to my great comfort, there appeared a cottage close to the road with a light in an upstairs window. I knocked loudly on the door and the lighted window was opened. A man's face appeared and he very irritably said, 'What d'ye want?' I said, 'Am I on the right road for Langford?' He barked out, 'Straight on,' and slammed the window.

Now, this wasn't at all satisfactory, for what was 'straight on'? He couldn't have known which way I had come, so ought I to turn back and follow in Sam's tracks or continue my own course? I was afraid to rouse him again and decided to carry on. Another half hour and to my joy I recognised the outlines of a farmhouse with outbuildings and was sure I was nearing home. Arrangements had been made for me to sleep in Sam's room that night on our return and although I was so weary I went on past father's cottage to the big house.

It was past midnight when I walked in alone to the astonishment of three of the maids who were waiting up for me and I had to tell them what I had done with Sam. Bless 'em, they gave me hot drink and a good supper and made me regard myself as a hero to have survived that long walk alone. Sam came in about an hour afterwards. He had gone several miles out of his road and looked quite 'done up'. Moreover, he was not fussed over one bit by the girls but was soundly berated for forsaking me!

At Mendip Lodge, I was escorted everywhere I went out of doors by the terrier 'Rattler', never a more faithful little chap than he was to me. My first duty in the morning was to fetch the milk from a farm situated quite near my parents' cottage and so I elected to go home to sleep every night no matter how late it was, so that I was saved that forward journey in the mornings. I couldn't let Rattler come with me for he was a good house dog and the maidservants insisted on keeping him in the house but the first of them to get about in the morning would let him out and he'd make a bee-line for our cottage where, if the door was shut, he'd give a peremptory bark for it to be opened.

I was very seldom up for I never got about half enough sleep for a growing lad and mother had much difficulty to get me on my legs – but when Rattler came on the scene she merely said, 'He's not up yet, you'd better fetch him.' Rattler would rush upstairs, spring on the bed barking and yelping, licking my face and making so much fuss that I was bound to get out of it. When we set off for the farm he'd always trot on ahead with his three inches of tail straight up and with such an important air, as much as to say, 'He'd never have rolled out but for me!'

Rattler was a great favourite with the girls in the house and after I left for the railway service, two of them took Rattler miles away to a good photographers, so that they could send me a photo of him. I still have it now.

SCHOOLBOY, SERVANT, GWR APPRENTICE

Some whims of the gentry

Before I entered his service Squire would sometimes drive a 'four in hand',[14] but I don't think his stables, in my time, contained four matched horses. He now decided to ride behind a postillion.[15] A strongly recommended lad was engaged, put into a fine suit of livery and, with a white lashed silver mounted whip, he looked smart and efficient, but his riding did not come up to Squire's standard.

One morning I was called out to the carriage drive by the butler. The squire and a horse held by a groom were there and to my surprise, I was helped on to the horse and told to ride up and down a short distance of the drive. I suppose they expected me to possess a born instinct to manage horses, father having been a lifelong coachman, but as I'd only done a little rough and ready riding, I have no doubt but that I cut a very poor figure on horseback. Anyhow, I did not want the postillion's job and very likely my expression and performance told them for I heard no more about it.

The would-be postillion was sacked and as it was found that his new livery coat just fitted me. It was handed over and when inclined, I could now sport three rows of silver buttons instead of the one which adorned my page's coat. Squire gave up his whim of having a postillion in his service.

Squire's sister[16] lived with him now and had a fancy for dogs but really no affection for them, just willing to part with them any time and acquire some other breed. I was detailed to care for her dogs. At first I had only one mongrel to look after and he was a poor specimen and had rather a rough time of it, for the gamekeeper who was often calling at the house, was always accompanied by a most aggressive terrier. Keeper claimed the dog's full name was 'Sir Richard Paget'[17] but this was shortened to 'Dick' for everyday use and the rascal would always pitch into my poor dog whenever they met up. Keeper wouldn't lift a hand to part them until my dog was chewed to a rag. A sociable old black retriever, another of Keeper's dogs, would look on as though it was only a matter of youngsters squabbling and no business of his.

Later our lady had a grand greyhound given her, 'Claude Duval'. I was told he was a famous courser till he came by a broken leg and although one could see no fault in the leg now, he was now out of show business.

Then she was presented with a beagle, 'Roger'. Now we were far too good for Keeper's dogs but Dick came along one day aggressive as ever and pitched into the young terrier but before he had half a bite, Claude Duval's great jaws clamped on him and I thought he'd be bitten in half. Keeper was quick enough to restore order now and by pushing his gun butt between them and shouting his loudest, he managed to get his beloved Dick away in one piece.

My lady took no interest in these three dogs and after about a year she gave away the greyhound and the beagle to her friends. She owned a pedigree Yorkshire terrier as well but this sissy dog was kept on velvet, had an ornamental wicker kennel and his meals given him at regular intervals, all consisting of the very best food.

One day, during a rainy period, I had orders to put on my livery top coat and top hat and was given a basket of 'goodies' to carry for I was to attend our lady and the Yorkshire terrier, 'Roly', by name, on a visit to several old cottagers. We came on a long stretch of muddy road and although I was carrying a fairly heavy basket, my lady turned to me and said, 'Pick up Roly, Alfred.' I had to manage somehow to get that little blighter under my unoccupied arm and carry him over this stretch of muddy road.

After the departure of the greyhound and beagle my lady bought a nearly full grown St. Bernard. I think it was sickening for distemper when it arrived. Anyhow, it soon had it and in spite of the vet's attention passed away. Then a Great Dane arrived, such a big spotted monster as was never seen in the neighbourhood before. Till it got better known all the women and children would keep as far away from it as possible but it was a most affectionate animal. This big chap was not in my care but was generally kept at the stables. He had his freedom and was often in and about the house. At this time a big lout of a chap brought the newspapers and periodicals daily to the house. He got to know the inoffensive nature of the dog and traded on it by pushing it aside and swearing at it.

One day the butler, on taking the newspapers from him, said, 'You'd better be more careful of that dog.' 'I ain't afraid of the d***ed old dog,' he insolently replied and walked away but after going a few yards shouted out another cheeky remark. Butler said to the Great Dane 'Get him!' In two bounds that dog was on him, knocking him down and standing over him –

but on Butler calling, he trotted back at once. That bad mannered lout of a news carrier had the scare of his life and slunk off without a word. Made a bit of extra work for me though, for he would never come up to the house again but left all papers at the nearest cottage and I had to fetch them from there.

On the subject of dogs, Alfred also recalls an incident when he was working at Mendip Lodge that brought him back into contact with his father's former employer, Evan Llewellyn. 'Squire' in the following story is therefore Evan Llewellyn rather than Benjamin Somers.

Squire's three dogs came up in the wood at Mendip Lodge disturbing the game. They were recognised as belonging to him and I was ordered to round them up and take them back to him at Langford Court. It was a very hot summer afternoon as I set off with five dogs, two of my employer's and the three disturbers of the peace.

I had almost reached the Court. I could see Squire sitting out on the lawn in the shade of a tree, apparently reading his paper. Then those dogs eyed a herd of pigs close to the ha-ha surrounding the front of the house – and at them they dashed. So did I, shouting and kicking at the dogs but they got one pig down and were savaging it when up rushed Squire. He threw a big heavy walking stick at the three actually worrying the fallen pig and by that, and our combined kicking and shouting, we managed to bring them to order – but we had had a most exciting ten minutes and were both very heated and almost breathless. As soon as he could speak Squire shouted, 'What the devil do you mean by bringing all these dogs along here?' For the first time I lost all awe of the powerful gentleman and shouted back, 'They're not my dogs, they're yours, been up to our place hunting and I had to bring them back!'

Squire looked critically at the chief culprits and said 'Hmm, hmm.' The anger faded from his face and he continued, 'You go on into the kitchen and get yourself something to eat and drink.' I wanted the drink, so obeyed readily enough and when the cook heard my tale she said 'Don't wonder at it. Our dogs are trained to drive those pigs off if they come near the lawn.'

It is slightly surprising that Squire Evan Llewellyn fails to recognise his own dogs but less surprising perhaps that, having realised his mistake, he offers Alfred no apology. This is the only overt showing of temper by Alfred in the whole memoir, although, as we have already seen, Alfred actually felt a respect and admiration for Evan Llewellyn that lasted for the whole of his life.

Alfred was rather less enamoured of the senior member of the family at Mendip Lodge, Benjamin Somers's elderly mother, Elizabeth, who was the direct employer of Alfred's father.

When the weather was fine Squire's mother liked to take slow walks along the carriage drive, one hand on my shoulder, the other using a slender walking stick. I had no standing orders for this business as it was so irregular and I had so much to do away from the house, feeding the peafowl, tending the fancy pheasants and so on, that I could always put up a good excuse for my absence.

When I left Mendip Lodge to enter the railway service, Squire's mother gave me a big gilt-edged leather bound *Church Service* with the remark, 'If you'd been more obedient to me I'd have given you far more than this.' What a present to give a lad of fifteen! But I don't doubt that by my neglect of her I suffered quite a substantial loss. The old lady lived to well on in the nineties, chiefly on a diet of rice pudding and baked apples which I carried up to her many a time in her private room.

The old lady had overbearing ways and expected servility from all working people. In fine weather she would often take the air in her big open carriage drawn by her two fine black horses. If he was available, the senior coachman would drive and my father would be in reserve by his side. My father was as nimble as any young man and I'm sure the old dame preferred his attention to these of anyone else when she entered or alighted from her carriage. She might have had the footman with her at any time but she never did. Thus she would make her visits and tour the countryside, bestowing a wintry smile on any cottager's wife who curtseyed to her or to any man who doffed his hat. I'm sure she regarded them as all very inferior to her aristocratic self. A pair of well-matched valuable horses, two men-servants in green livery coats, white breeches, top hats and top boots, all to impress the importance of the little old lady in her fine carriage on the country folk.

I never felt so enraged at a member of the aristocracy as I did one summer evening. My father, as coachman, had brought the dowager lady home from a dinner party when a thunderstorm, which had been threatening for hours, broke out in extreme violence a few minutes after he had delivered the old lady safe indoors.

It seems almost unbelievable but that old baggage sent out orders that my father was to walk back to the house that she had been visiting to inform the inmates that she had arrived safely. We other servants all strongly advised father to wait till the storm abated but he knew that old lady. His job depended on promptly carrying out her orders, so off he went in the storm, the duration and violence of which was talked of for years afterwards. A two mile walk by the nearest footpaths and except during the lightning flashes, it was now pitch dark.

Yet a year or so later that same old dame, hearing that my brother had won a scholarship and was entering college, gave my father ten pounds (a princely sum in those days) to provide all necessary books and clothes to start him off in a fitting manner.[18] However, I took a great dislike to her for ordering my father out the night of that great storm.

Alfred moves on

One day when I was near sixteen years of age my mistress said to me it was time I left her service to better myself and what would I like to do, for she would pay a premium for me to be apprenticed to any trade I fancied.[19]

Now what a simpleton I was! I had no idea of railway work and had only once in my life been in a train.[20] The nearest railway station was over four miles from our village, yet I told her I wished to 'go on the railway'. She wrote off to Head Office and received a reply that they had no vacancy at present in our district but would advise her later.

A fortnight passed without a call for my services and our lady asked me again if I would not prefer to be apprenticed and I agreed to enter the building trade. On receipt of a note, the most prosperous builder in the neighbourhood readily agreed to come to the house next morning at 10.00 a.m. bringing the necessary form that would bind me apprentice – but at 9.30 a.m., my lady opened a letter from the Great Western Railway Head Office requesting that I should report to their Bristol Office next morning.

A groom was sent off post-haste to save the builder a fruitless errand and by that half-hour my destiny was decided. It was the G.W.R. for me. Later, when I missed all the comforts of home and the good living I had got used to, didn't I regret it!

I had to present two references to the railway officials. The one from my present employer was handed to me at once and in the afternoon I went off to the vicarage to get the other. The parson knew me right from christening time and all through my school career. I had waited on him many times when he had his legs under Squire's table. He greeted me very affably. He probably thought I was carrying an invitation for him to dinner but on hearing my request for a reference he said, 'You don't want to go on the railway. Come in here.' He opened the door of a spare room where there were several big trunks and some cases. 'There,' said he. 'If you go on the railway you will have to cart such loads as that about. You go back to school and follow in your brother's footsteps but if after thinking it over, you are still determined to enter the railway service come to me again.'

I knew his advice could not be followed. Grand parents I had, self sacrificing all the years we youngsters were growing up and now Edward, having won a scholarship, was away at college. It was a big strain on them to find the necessary cash to buy books and clothes, and to provide him with a little pocket money. So how could I add to their burden? No, it couldn't be done. I must be self-supporting.

Our Member of Parliament lived about two miles away and on leaving the vicarage I made a bee line for his residence.[21] I was lucky enough to catch him at home and was shown into his presence at once. He knew me well for he was a frequent visitor at the Squire's house and all the gentry round about had a smile for Squire's page boy. No hesitation with him. As soon as I had stated my business he sat down at his desk and wrote me out an excellent reference. I have it now, dated June 18th 1890.

The ruins of Mendip Lodge as they are today – overgown and completely hidden in woodland. The demolition of Mendip Lodge in the 1950s was, by all accounts, undertaken by the army, who used the building for target practice. (David Wilkins)

FAMILY AND CIRCUMSTANCES, 1890

Alfred

Alfred, now aged 16, has been encouraged by his former employer, the Somers family of Mendip Lodge, Burrington, to leave service and take up an apprenticeship. He has been offered a place by the GWR where he will work for two years as a 'lad porter' – a type of trainee – before becoming a permanent member of GWR uniformed staff at the age of 18, assuming his progress has been satisfactory.

To take up his new job, Alfred must leave his home village to live 12 miles away in the village of Worle, near Weston-super-Mare, where he is to be employed at the tiny village station. The job title of 'lad porter' seems, incidentally, to have been misleading in a similar way to that of 'pageboy'. Although Alfred's job does involve some portering for passengers, as might be expected, he also functions as a general odd-job boy and is required to undertake many other duties including building repairs, maintenance of signalling lamps, assisting the signalman, operating the telegraph, delivering parcels around the village and so on.

In Worle, Alfred takes lodgings with John and Ann Watts, a couple in their 60s who live in a cottage near the Old King's Head Inn at The Scores (now The Scaurs), a lane in the village. John Watts also works for the GWR as foreman to a gang of labourers.

Worle

Worle has since been wholly absorbed by the outward development of Weston-super-Mare and is now a suburb of the town. In 1890, when Alfred

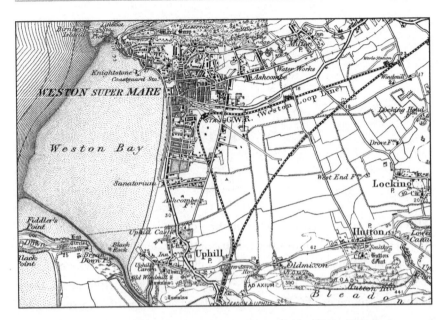

Late nineteenth-century map showing the Weston Loop diverting from the Bristol to Exeter main line to pass through the town before rejoining the main line a short distance on.

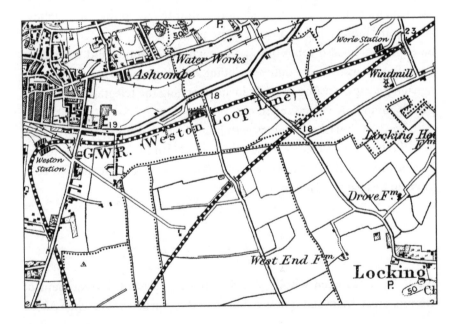

lived there, it was still a distinct, small village, 2 or 3 miles inland from Weston and surrounded on all sides by woodland and fields.

Weston-super-Mare

Weston-super-Mare had grown from being a village of around thirty houses at the beginning of the nineteenth century to, in 1890, a small but thriving seaside resort with hotels, a pier, cafés and other entertainments for visitors. This growth and prosperity was a direct result of Weston's connection to the main-line railway built by the Bristol and Exeter Railway in the 1840s. Weston's extensive, sandy beach had made it an attractive destination for day-trippers and works outings. Train-travelling, summer fun-seekers came to Weston not just from Bristol but from as far away as the Midlands.

Worle Station and the Weston Loop

The Bristol and Exeter Railway had amalgamated with the GWR in 1876 and was now part of the GWR's route from London to Penzance. The main line passed within a couple of miles of Weston-super-Mare but Weston was not, strictly speaking, a main-line station. Instead the town's connection was (and still is) on a 'loop' line.

A loop line leaves the main line at one point and rejoins it at another. A train can either travel straight along the main line, ignoring the loop, or it can take the loop before returning to the main line and continuing along it.

A loop gives the train operator flexibility with the timetable. In this case, for example, more trains would be scheduled to take the loop via Weston in the summer when the line was busy with day-trippers than in the winter when it was not. A further benefit for Weston was that its proximity to Bristol

Opposite below: The location of Worle Station on the Weston Loop, immediately after the junction between the loop line and the main line (see top-right corner of map). Just above Worle Station on the opposite side of the line is the signal box at Worle Junction. The main line and the signal box are both within a short walk of Worle Station.

This photograph was taken much later than the period of the memoir but it gives an excellent indication of the physical layout of Worle Junction. The train is just rejoining the main line from the loop line and is travelling north towards Bristol. Worle Station can be seen at the tail end of the train. Worle Junction Signal Box is just visible, situated in the 'V' of the junction. (Worle History Society)

allowed GWR to terminate trains there instead of at Bristol Temple Meads. This helped the GWR by freeing up space in Bristol and had the incidental effect of 'providing Weston-super-Mare with a lavish passenger service that it otherwise would never have had'.[1]

The Weston Loop was only 6 miles long. Besides Weston-super-Mare Station itself, the only other station on the loop was the tiny village station at Worle where Alfred was to be based. Worle Station was situated immediately after the loop-line junction in the southbound direction.

3

ALFRED PLUMLEY

GWR APPRENTICE

'The mighty GWR'

It is difficult now to grasp the sheer speed and magnitude of the social change brought about by the development of railways in Britain in the middle of the nineteenth century.

Before the coming of the railways, when Alfred's grandfather was a boy, the ability to move people and things around Britain was pretty much the same as it had been for centuries. The development of the inland waterway network had improved the transportation of goods, but perishable foodstuffs – to take just one very simple example – still could not be taken very far. Most people still ate produce from local farms while seated at tables made by local carpenters in houses built from local materials. Human travel was largely restricted to the speed and distance it was practicable to walk or to journeys that could be made on horseback or by horse-drawn vehicle. The great majority of ordinary people never travelled further than a few miles in their lifetime and had no expectation or ambition that they might do otherwise.

The first inkling that this long-established normality was about to be swept away came in 1830. On 15 September of that year the world's first steam passenger railway, the Liverpool & Manchester, opened for business and in no time at all the country found itself in the grip of what quickly became known as 'Railway Mania'. Over the next two or three decades hundreds of railway routes would be proposed by excited entrepreneurs in possession of a map, a pencil and crucially, for the straight lines, a ruler. Numerous speculative railway companies were established. Some hoped to construct great sweeping routes that would enable passengers to travel distances previously unimaginable at speeds previously unbelievable; others of these companies wished to do nothing more ambitious than connect a single colliery or stone quarry to the nearest town.

In 1833, in Bristol, a group of local merchants observed Liverpool's embrace of this new-fangled transport technology with some anxiety. They realised that the railway line from Liverpool to Birmingham, which had just then been given the go-ahead by government, would provide a connection to the Birmingham to London line that was already under construction. At a stroke, Liverpool would then have a fast, direct link to London and might easily depose their own city as England's most important west-coast port. This was an existential threat to Bristol's future prosperity. The group needed to act, and the solution was obvious: they would establish a railway company of their own. Thus, the Great Western Railway was born.

The founders of the GWR were ambitious. They wanted the finest, most up-to-date railway service in the country. The urgent need was, of course, to link Bristol to London but the long-term intention was to connect other towns and cities in the south-west of England both to the capital and to each other. In a defining stroke of genius, the founding group appointed as chief engineer to their new enterprise a man who was to become one of the greatest public figures of the nineteenth century – Isambard Kingdom Brunel (1806–59).

Brunel was simultaneously a grand-scale visionary and a practical nuts-and-bolts man. These two strands of his personality came together in his willingness to develop bold, new methods to tackle the technical challenges thrown up by Victorian industrial growth. Brunel was comfortable as a civil engineer, a mechanical engineer and a building engineer. For the GWR, he would design elegant viaducts and bridges, and build grand and beautiful stations. He was undaunted by the scale of the earth-moving projects entailed in building a railway from scratch and was willing to take on such natural obstacles as Box Hill, between Chippenham and Bath, through which he drove what was then the world's longest tunnel.

In keeping with his reputation for innovation, Brunel decided at the outset of his time with the GWR that that the company should operate a 'broad-gauge' railway – that is to say that its tracks would be 7ft¼in wide, by comparison with the width of 4ft 8½in that was becoming standard elsewhere in the country. This wider gauge, Brunel argued, would allow the GWR's passenger trains to travel more quickly and more smoothly than trains on the narrower gauge systems. It would also enable goods trains to haul bigger trucks.

Immediately on his appointment to the GWR, Brunel set to work surveying the south of England. He chose a more northerly route between London and Bristol than might have seemed obvious but one which was generally flatter and which offered useful connections. Construction of the line from the new station at Paddington in London began in 1836 and progressed rapidly. It reached Bristol in 1841 having connected to Maidenhead, Reading, Swindon and Bath en route.

Once the line reached Bristol it was immediately connected to the new broad-gauge line being built southwards by the Bristol & Exeter Railway (this company was one of several independent railway companies that had working agreements with the GWR). By 1849, passengers could make an unbroken journey all the way from London to Plymouth. In 1867, the main line arrived in Penzance at the tip of Cornwall, finally running out of landscape to conquer.

The coming of the railways changed forever people's attitude to distance. Within a few decades it had become possible for more or less anyone to start from anywhere in the country and end up more or less wherever they fancied going. This radical social development led, among other things, to new ways of thinking about leisure. The GWR in particular, with its several routes to the south-west coast, was instrumental in creating a social phenomenon - the seaside holiday. Even in the nineteenth century when working people had far fewer days off work each year, the GWR's passenger trains, with their carriages in elegant chocolate and cream livery, were crowded on summer weekends with day-trippers headed for resorts like Minehead, Weymouth, Newquay, Torquay and Dawlish.

By 1890, the year when Alfred decided on a whim to throw in his lot with the railway, the GWR was operating on a monumental scale. It had been defeated in the 'Gauge War' and was in the process of converting its broad-gauge lines to the narrower gauge track that now dominated the railway system nationally, but - that one setback aside - the GWR was as thriving an example of British business as can be imagined. Astute management had allowed it to absorb a number of other railway companies and, with its almost 1,900 miles of track, it had become the largest railway company in Britain. The other major railway companies were content with one main line each but the GWR had three. In addition to the original London to Bristol line, there was now a cross-country line from London to New Milford in west Wales via the towns and cities of the Welsh Valleys, and another from London to Birkenhead via Birmingham. The GWR also owned or managed numerous smaller railways systems and branch lines throughout its heartland in the south-west.

It was to one of the very most obscure backwaters of this great network that Alfred had been posted as a 'lad porter'. But first he had to negotiate the administrative process of his new appointment by travelling alone to Bristol ...

Lost in Bristol – and an embarrassing encounter with a medical man

That morning[1] I was up and off about 7.00 a.m. to catch the 8.00 train (a four mile walk). I wasn't encumbered with any clothes but those I stood up in, my parents thinking it best to retain my box of belongings and forward it on when they knew where I was appointed.

On arrival in town, after making several enquiries, I found the right office. I was asked a few questions by an official and then given a note addressed to a doctor in Redcliffe Hill. I had never been in town before on my own and was feeling pretty confused by the traffic and had much difficulty in finding the doctor's residence but reached it at last. I was shown into the presence of a big, elderly man who glanced at the note I handed him and then barked out, 'Get those clothes off.' After a body examination he pointed through a window to where a weathercock was visible about a quarter of a mile away and asked, 'Which way is the wind?' I replied, 'Northerly, sir.' He fairly bellowed at me, 'I don't mean that. Which way is the wind?' I extended my arm and said, 'That way.' 'Then why didn't you say so?' he grunted. He then wrote a short note which he gave to me and I was very relieved to find myself out in the street again.[2]

Worle – working life on a country station

Apparently the doctor's report was satisfactory for, on presenting it to the railway official, I was given a brown paper parcel and a pass to the country station at Worle, near Weston-super-Mare, where I was to take up my duties. The Station Master, Mr Emanuel Day, told another lad porter to take me up to the village and see if I could be accepted at his lodging. The motherly old landlady, Mrs Watts, accepted me at once; seven shillings a week, plus sevenpence for a two-course Sunday dinner. This left me with the princely sum of 1*sh*/5*d* to spend on all the other necessaries of life.

I was a sad, disappointed lad that night for I had opened my brown paper parcel in the privacy of my bedroom to find that the contents were a soiled second-hand suit of corduroy and uniform cap. I, who had been wearing best tailor-made clothes for the last four years, to be reduced to this! I shed a few tears.

Surprising to say, this despised suit was not a bad fit and next morning I attended at the station as a uniformed servant of the mighty G.W.R. It was a beautiful country district, the very best time of year, and the novelty of new faces and entirely different work soon drove away any depression for I was determined to make good.

Mr Day was a dear old chap in his sixties, a most worthy man, respected by all who knew him. I was soon on excellent terms with him. He was more of a farmer than a railwayman. He rented several fields, kept a horse, cows, pigs, many poultry and cultivated a very big garden. He was quite useless with a pen and the senior porter had to do all station accounts but he would make any article of wickerwork or do a job of carpentry or tin-smithing as expertly as a skilled tradesman. For the hard work in connection with his little farm he kept a man in constant employment.

I might have been sent to many a worse place. Our station was most pleasantly situated. We had an unobstructed view of the main line about twenty yards distant, along which the world famous broad gauge G.W.R. expresses rolled majestically on their journeys to and from the West Country.

The senior porter put me wise as to my duties; sweep out the office and waiting rooms was the first bit of business, then be on the alert to see the milk carts arrive, collecting the consignment notes and helping to load up the station barrows, from which to book up the cans to destination. It was always a bit of a bustle till the first up-train had left the station.

My next job was to walk the line for nearly a mile in three different directions to bring in the signal lamps. The main line junction[3] was close by but our station was situated just inside, on the loop line. Lamps claimed a lot of attention from me. Signal and platform lamps had to be kept scrupulously clean, the cases polished up with cotton waste and whiting. Climbing the high iron ladder was a bit terrifying at first, for up top on the double-armed post, the little platform would sway about as if very inclined to topple over. One actually did topple over some short time after I left this station and my successor was so scared that he left the service at once.

The carriages were lighted by colza oil-burning lamps, some of which gave out about as much light as a hardworking glow-worm.[4] A trolley-load of trimmed lamps, attended by two men, would be wheeled alongside a train. One man would mount to the top of the end carriage and, walking along the roofs, take a lamp, hoisted up on a pole by his mate and drop it in

The lane in Worle, known as The Scores, where Alfred found lodgings with Mrs Watts in a cottage near the Old King's Head Inn. The white gable end wall of the Old King's Head is visible at the top of the hill. (Post 1890, Worle History Society)

the cavity provided for it and so proceed for the whole length of the train. Heating was only done by large flat metal hot water footwarmers, often very battered and never very hot. If you wanted a really hot one the only way to get it was to tip a porter to get one direct from the boiler house.

On market day it was the usual thing to have several calves mooing away on the platform. Their bodies and legs would be encased in sacks, a tie round the neck keeping each sack in position – one shilling each for carriage to town if accompanied by the owner. We had only two four wheeled trolleys and when they were full all other goods had to be lifted up into the train from the platform – a foot-high lift. Seventeen-gallon cans of milk[5] and full grown calves were about as much as we two lad porters could manage.

I had been supplied with a new corduroy uniform now and I often wondered why it was so saturated with green dye when issued. If one rubbed a hand down it, the hand would be coloured and any white material that touched it would need to go into the wash-tub. Every man's official number must be displayed on his coat sleeve, in red figures on an oval tab. The general belief was that this number enabled passengers to report any incivility received from the wearer. Some men strongly objected to this label but personally, I rather think it was a good thing. I carried the number 15718, first on my sleeve, then later on the collar of a tunic and always saw it on the paybill of my nearly forty-five years of service. I was never ashamed of it but the display of numbers was abolished when the issue of serge uniforms became general.

During the summer months we were very busy, for all excursion trains to Weston-super-Mare called at our station on the forward journey for the collection of tickets. One or two full time ticket collectors came to help us and we would often collect several thousands a day, all of which had to be sorted in numerical order, tied up in bundles and despatched to the Railway Audit Office next day.[6]

My fellow lad porter and I were directed to spend a short time each day in the signal cabin to learn the single needle telegraph.[7] The signalman on duty never objected to our presence. All he cared about was for us to become familiar with the recognised call for this, the Main Line Junction Cabin for then when he had a few minutes' interval between trains he would, weather

One of very few available photographs of Worle Station, none of which shows the station when it was actually open (it closed in 1922 but was not demolished until the 1960s). This photograph shows the abandoned station, sometime in the 1940s or 1950s. The platform seems to have been fenced off, perhaps for safety reasons. (Worle History Society)

permitting, put in a bit of work in his nearby garden. All the bell rings were audible to him when in the garden but not the faint sounds made by the single needle telegraph. One of we lads would be left in charge with orders to shout out as soon as a call came through.

The single needle telegraph was quite a nightmare to many of the old signalmen, they just could not 'pick it up' and as the only instrument provided to a country station was generally situated in the signal box, any lad with such a superficial knowledge as I possessed was often in demand.

Alfred's time at Worle Station continued in this happy vein, as we shall see, but – as in the case of the fatal fire that occurred in his childhood – there was no escaping the fact that sudden death was commonplace during this period. Like all heavy industry prior to the establishment of trade unions and the demands for safer working conditions, the railway could be a dangerous place. In the middle of his pleasant memories of his time at Worle, Alfred reminds us of this.

One morning my mate strained himself in helping to lift a seventeen gallon can of milk from the platform into the train and in consequence had to go on the sick list. In his absence, Station Master engaged a lad from the village, a cheerful, willing young chap. When the lad left our station he was given temporary employment at Weston-super-Mare and there, in carrying out his duties, he was crushed to death between the buffers of a train. His parents, who lived next door to my lodging, were about heartbroken by the loss of their only son in such a tragic manner.[8]

Although Worle is only around 12 miles from his home village of Langford, the length of Alfred's working week made it very difficult for him to find the time to visit his family. That must have been tough for a lad of 16 who had never lived away from home before and who was so fond of his mum and dad. The problem of limited time was compounded by the rather circuitous train route, which almost doubled the distance, and the 4-mile walk between Alfred's parents' cottage and the nearest station.

Very little I saw of my parents or native place after I entered the G.W.R. service for although I was never stationed at any great distance away, the four mile walk to my parents' home from the nearest station was a great obstacle to overcome in the very short times I was free. It was just a bare Sunday free. No week-ends except as a very special favour.

There were no regular 'privilege tickets' for railway employees in those days and when I did wish to go home for the weekend – about twenty five miles away by rail – fatherly old Mr Day would ask the guard of the chosen train to, 'Just see this lad past the ticket collector at the Junction' and I travelled free, for I was known at my local station as a company's servant and no questions asked.

One Sunday, a village lad with whom I had become very friendly made arrangements with me to walk to and from my home, taking the very shortest route across country, which made the journey only about half the distance it was by rail. We got there all right, had a good dinner and after an early tea set off on our return. Two very weary lads rolled into port that night and both were very decidedly of the opinion that there would not be a second attempt.

The signal cabin at Worle Junction in 1892. The passing train is the Cornishman Express pulled by broad-gauge locomotive *Inkermann*. (Rev. A.H. Malan / Great Western Trust)

There was always the compensation of a visit to the seaside though. If my mate or I wanted to have an hour or so at Weston-super-Mare we got through on the nod, for we found that old Charlie the ticket collector was very fond of mushrooms. By taking him a packet or two in the season, he would pass us by for the rest of the year!

A proper winter

Alfred's posting to Worle coincided with one of the most severe British winters on record. An intense frost affecting the whole country began in late November 1890 and continued without any let up until late January 1891.[9] December 1890 remains the coldest December ever recorded, with an average temperature that remained below freezing across the entire country for the whole month.[10]

A spell of mild weather followed, giving the impression perhaps that the worst was over but, towards the end of the first week in March, the bitterly cold weather suddenly returned. Then, on the evening of Monday 9 March a howling blizzard began, initially across the south-west of England and south Wales and eventually spreading across the whole of southern England. Hurricane-force winds struck Cornwall, Devon and Somerset with snow so thick in the air that people could barely see. These unusual and quite frightening conditions lasted in varying degrees for four days. Extensive damage was caused to property and up to half a million trees are believed to have been brought down. In the English Channel, at least sixty-three ships were wrecked with 220 people drowned.[11] Many people were trapped by the snow. Near Penzance, to take just one of scores of reported examples, passengers on a horse-drawn omnibus were forced to remain inside the vehicle for three days when it could make no further progress in the snow.[12]

The railways were particularly badly affected by the severe weather. Snow was said to have completely filled some railway cuttings and dozens of trains

Staff of Weston-super-Mare Station in the 1890s. 'Old Charlie', the mushroom-loving ticket collector, may well be among those shown, as may young George Sperring who was killed in an accident at the station. (STEAM – Museum of the GWR, Swindon)

were stranded overnight, either by fallen trees or impassable snowdrifts. Many passengers were forced to abandon stuck trains and struggle to nearby villages through snow that was often well above waist height. In some cases passengers were reported as having to walk along on the hedge tops. Clothes froze to people's backs.[13]

At the height of the snowstorm, the GWR is reported to have had fifty-one passenger trains and thirteen goods trains unable to move.[14] In the most famous case, the GWR's Zulu Express, which left London for Plymouth at 3 p.m. on 9 March, became trapped in a snowdrift on Dartmoor. Some historians suggest that the train ground to a halt in open moorland and was eventually completely buried by snow. It was said to be two days before a farmer noticed the top of the funnel protruding from the drift and arranged for help.[15] Others suggest that the train halted at the tiny Dartmoor station of Brent, unable to proceed any further.[16] Either way, the experience must have been truly appalling for both passengers and crew. It was days before the train was dug out by teams of navvies and it did not make it to Plymouth until eight days after it had left London. Not surprisingly, this remains the most delayed British train journey on record. Some passengers, showing true British phlegm, were reported to have stayed onboard for the entire journey.

Anyone struggling to carry on with their life during such extraordinary weather was unlikely to forget the experience. Alfred was no exception.

The evening of the great snow storm I managed to get all my signal lamps lighted and up on their posts before it got too bad, then I was sent off to the village to call out the 'fogmen' who were urgently required on duty to help in signalling the trains.

What a job it was! There was a terrific wind and heavy blinding snow. It was a real relief to get in the lee of a house and recover one's breath. I wasn't a welcome visitor, for no-one would venture out on such a night unless compelled to do so. However, when I had delivered my message I'd done my duty and the poor fogman had to leave his fireside and turn out in the raging blizzard and do his.

Next morning I left my lodging about 7.00 a.m. and just outside the village there was a horse and milk-cart nearly buried in the snow. The driver was just returning home to get help and tools to dig the poor horse and loaded cart out. It was sheer madness ever to have made the attempt to get the milk through to the station. I floundered on and overtook Mr Day who said, 'You go on if you can, you're younger than me'.

What hedges there were, were completely buried. It was just one smooth expanse of snow except for an isolated tree here and there – but the chief danger were the deep rhines which bordered each side of the road for about a half mile.[17] Now I'd passed Station Master there were no footsteps for me to follow, and under such conditions, a slip into the rhine would be fatal. I got safely to the station but need not have hurried for there were no trains over the loop that day or the next.

All work was centred on clearing the main line which was blocked in the down direction. A snow plough had arrived in the night and gone ahead to clear the way but had itself got derailed. A couple of expresses were held up at the Junction waiting to proceed but it was some hours before an up-train came through.

GWR locomotive *Leopard* derailed at Camborne in Cornwall during the great blizzard of 1891. (Great Western Trust)

Snow or no snow I had to have my signal lamps trimmed and burning. There were strict orders that they had to be fetched in every morning, trimmed and replaced in their cases on the signal every evening before dusk. I broke the rule that day and the following one by taking a can of oil round and filling them up at the posts, lighting and replacing them at once, for one journey a day through that deep snow was enough for anyone.

I cannot be sure now whether it was before or after this heavy snow fall that we had three weeks of continuous hard frost[18] when one could take the heaviest road vehicle on the ice over any of the ponds – or 'pits' as they were locally called in that part of the country.

I had a most unpleasant experience one morning. During the long severe frost I had been in the habit of going from the Branch Distant Signal across the fields to get the lamp from the Main Distant Signal as this was much the shortest way. This could only be done during a severe frost as it was necessary to cross a deep rhine on the ice. All went well during this period but eventually the thaw set in and I had to tramp the line in each direction again. Then, later in the winter, we had another spell of frost and ice on all the water. I decided on trying my short cut again. Coming to the rhine I very gingerly ventured onto the ice. It appeared to be strong enough so over I went and was taking the very last step to the safety of the other side when – crash! In I went, well above the waist line.

Luckily, by grasping the strong reed growing on the side I kept in an upright position and managed to scramble out. That ice-cold water was some shock. It was freezing hard and within a minute or two my wet clothes were a mass of glittering ice as I hurried back to the station. A few words of explanation to Station Master and I was off to my lodging. The heat of my body melted the ice before I reached the village so that I didn't look such a strange spectacle as I had. A good rub down and some dry clothing put me fit for duty again but I was taking no more 'short cuts' over the rhine after that.

A station in the countryside

As we have seen, although Weston-super-Mare had been expanding since the construction of the railway, it was still a relatively small town and Worle was still a small village, surrounded by fields and woodland. Worle Station was situated a little way from the centre of the village in a completely rural setting where, as a country lad himself, Alfred presumably felt pretty much at home. The memoir conveys a sense of the station building – and even the railway itself – as a benign presence, at ease with the gentle rhythm of the surrounding countryside and village life.

Although water was so plentiful in the neighbourhood, it was only that drawn from deep wells that was passed as fit for drinking. We had a pump at the station but the water was unfit for drinking and this lack of pure water was much deplored all through the hot summer.

Our landlady made a big brew of tea each morning and filled a tin can each for her husband and we two lodgers and these cans were warmed up by a fire when we wanted a drink. The cans were rinsed out every night and at weekends boiled out – but long before the Saturday they were very foul and I wonder that the contents didn't poison us! We should have been much wiser to have provided ourselves with a water bottle filled at the village pump which stood just across the road from our lodging but the tea-can habit had been in force for so many years that our old landlady would have had a shock if we had declined it.

Through the apple season and in autumn, apples and cyder were to be had for the asking, and more often than not the old lady's cans were emptied out on the ground. We had a good oven grate in the porter's room and for several months in the year the oven would daily contain either baked apples or potatoes for both could be obtained within a few yards of the door. Such addition to our diet no doubt helped to keep us healthy.

The station did not boast of much in the flower line. We had no proper flower beds as so many other country stations were so proud of but there was a good excuse for us, for in the summer our platforms were often crowded by excursionists and any flowers smaller than a dinner plate would have been carried off!

Station Master did the best he could under the circumstances. Every spring he would plant sunflower seeds in boxes and as soon as he thought there was no risk of further frost he, assisted by one of us lad porters, would make holes through the gravelled platform a few inches from the palings with an iron bar and put a young sunflower plant in it, filling up the hole with a good soil. These plants did remarkably well, none under six feet in height when full grown and all bearing the usual great yellow petalled flowers. There was a stretch of glass-roofed verandah in the front of the station and from the timber supports were suspended flower baskets filled with ivy leaved geraniums and that was all the floral display we made.

There was a shallow pit bordered by the station down-platform railings and there being no entrance or exit from this platform except over the line, the pit was very seldom visited. One beautiful spring morning I climbed over the palings to explore this bit of secluded property. I found that the pit was nearly dry and, by proceeding cautiously, one could wander all over it dry-footed. To my surprise, about every little tump of coarse grass or reed contained a coot's or moorhen's nest, every one holding a number of eggs. There must have been hundreds of them.

What an artful shy lot these water birds were! Only the station railings between them and the noisy trains, the station staff and the passengers so often on the platform yet they were carrying on all their domestic affairs and arranging to bring another generation of their kind into the world and no-one was aware of their existence so close till I took my short morning ramble. Even then I didn't see a single bird! We knew there were plenty in the neighbourhood, for on the deeper pits they might be seen any time sporting on the water and if one approached close they would either dive or flutter into the bordering rushes to creep furtively through them to a safer place. If one cared to wait, very quietly, for a few minutes, they would reappear but very rarely at the point where they went into hiding.

Our Station Master always went home about seven o'clock and many long winter evenings we lads spent at the station. Our passengers were few and far between and we had the lighted, warmed buildings practically to ourselves. We might have had a score of village youths for company but always limited ourselves to about six respectable boys. With one of these friends I bought a set of second-hand boxing gloves and a half dozen of us (my fellow porter consenting) would meet in the station's Waiting Room and plug away at each other. Only two of us had ever put on the gloves when we started and we were very amused at the funny ideas the others had of fistic combat.

We were even daring enough to invite in several young ladies of our acquaintance and tried a bit of dancing. But a few evenings proved sufficient. You can't trust the ladies and rumours got around, so we cut out all ladies' company at once. I really had no business there, for I was booked off duty at 7.00 p.m. and the senior porter was alone on duty. If any tales of slackness had got to our Mr Day's ears we should have been 'for it' – but I never knew him to visit the station in the evening after he had left it at 7.00 p.m. and he lived nearly a mile away.

Our little gatherings broke up as longer days approached and outdoor games became popular. There were no Saturday afternoons free then, and on Bank Holidays one was lucky to leave duty after twelve or fourteen hours. I have done eighteen on a specially heavy public holiday, starting again after five hours' rest. It was very vexing to me that I could never be free on a Saturday afternoon, as the majority of lads were, and consequently I could never take part in any of those afternoon matches in which luckier fellows than myself found much interest and pleasure.

The man who did the gardening and farm work for Station Master when I was porter under at Worle was a long lanky chap of eighteen, kind and good-tempered as they make 'em. He and I were soon good pals. I was fond of wrestling and although Jim was older, taller and stronger than I, I found I could put him on the floor every time. I would just rush at him and, embracing him on a low tackle, give him a bit of a heave and he'd shut up just like a jackknife and down we'd go, I always arranging to be on top. Then one day as I approached him, Jim deliberately sat down. 'What for?' says I. 'Ah,' says he, 'if I'm down you can't put me down and it's softer going.' In this simple way Jim put an end to our wrestling.

Mr Day was like a father to Jim and me, and declared he'd make handy-men of us. I have no doubt but what he would have done in time but Head Office moved me on before I picked up lots that he could – and would – have taught me. He started in teaching Jim gardening, the care of livestock, thatching and rough carpentry and I guess he made him a handy-man for he was shaping very well when I left.

I remember one time when the cowshed needed thatching. The reed was all in readiness (there was, when in season, always an abundance to be obtained from nearby pits). Mr Day had given Jim practical instruction how to perform the work and then left him to it. A little later, having a bit of leisure, I walked over to see if Jim was doing it to my satisfaction. He was up on the roof. I climbed the short ladder and one of his feet being invitingly near, I gave it a sharp tug and Jim slithered by me on his way to the ground, taking an armful of reed with him.

It was only about a foot drop and soft landing but Jim appeared to be very upset and said some words such as one pal shouldn't use to another and I told him so. He was still throwing reflections on my character when a stern voice said, 'What's all this mess, James?' There was Station Master glowering at us. Jim pointed an accusing finger at me. ''Twas he, sir. He came up on the roof and pulled me down.' Then why didn't 'ee knock him down first?' roared the old gent. Without waiting for an answer he turned to me. 'You go on back to station. I'll talk to you later!' I obeyed, not a bit frightened. I knew the dear old chap's ways. No doubt he gave Jim a few sizzling remarks and that was all we'd hear of the matter.

It was no infrequent occurrence for animals to fall into the deep rhines nearby. I saw a heavy horse got out one day. His hooves were deeply embedded in the muddy bottom and the water was just over his back so it was quite impossible for the animal to move. A couple of men with spades cut the bank away down to the level of the water then a rope was thrown over his hindquarters and by gentle pulling by another horse, the bogged animal was got on to dry ground again.

My mate and I found it was quite easy to catch small eels in the pits. By looking along the sides where the water was clear of weeds one could see holes in the clay bottom about the size of a sixpence. It was necessary only to drop a worm-baited hook on one of these holes and almost immediately it would be drawn down out of sight. Wait a few seconds, then pull up and nearly always you'd have an eel – never a big one, youngsters, six inches to a foot in length. We caught many in this way but as our landlady forbade us to bring an eel (she called them 'water snakes') into the house we didn't follow this pastime for long.

An elderly man who lived near the village made a part-time business of eel-catching. He had wicker traps which he put down in the rhines in the evenings, taking them up at daybreak, and sending his catch off to a merchant in town. He told me the price he received. I thought it was very good and told him so. 'Ah, so 'tis,' he agreed, 'but I don't know that it pays. Look how I'm crippled with the rheumatics through getting wet so often.'

One evening I saw two men 'balling' for eels.[19] They had a long rod. On the end of it was a ball of worms. Each worm was threaded on strong worsted before being rolled into a ball about the size of a cricket ball, attached to the rod and slowly dragged along the bottom of a rhine, river or pond. If the fisherman felt a tug, he would expect to succeed in jerking an eel out on dry land, its teeth being caught up in the worsted. I never tried this game. There were sometimes some fine tench in the pits. I had weighed one on the station scales once for a lucky angler – seven pounds. He was very proud of his catch and well might be for it was a fine fish.

Give my regards to broad gauge

As we have seen, while Isambard Kingdom Brunel's championing of the broad-gauge railway system may have made sense from an engineering point of view, it had the disadvantage of placing the GWR at odds with the rest of the country, where all the existing lines had been laid in narrower gauge of what was to become the standard size.

Initially, it had not seemed to matter very much that two different gauges were in use but, as more new railway lines were built, the number of places where the two different gauges came together gradually increased. The public and politicians began to question the wisdom of a system that required passengers to disembark from a train of one gauge in order to continue their journey on a train of another gauge. Similarly, it was clearly a waste of resources to have to transfer goods between trucks of different gauges at places where the two gauges came together.

In 1845, parliament established the Gauge Commission to investigate ways of solving the problem. The commission recommended that broad gauge should be allowed to continue, but that its future use should be restricted entirely to the south-west of England. This recommendation became law in the Regulating the Gauge of Railways Act 1846.

These new regulations made it certain that broad-gauge lines would never become national standard. The effective outcome for the GWR was that it must either swap to the standard gauge or be forever condemned to operating a minority system that caused inconvenience to passengers, other railway operators and ultimately to itself. The writing was on the wall. The GWR gradually began to convert either to standard gauge or in some cases to a 'mixed-gauge' set up, which allowed trains of both gauges to travel along the same lines.

The complete conversion process took almost three decades. Fittingly, perhaps, the last line to convert to standard gauge (via a period as mixed gauge) was the GWR's grand, pioneering main line from London to Penzance via Bristol. On 20 May 1892 – less than a year into Alfred's employment with the GWR – the last ever broad-gauge train left Paddington for the far end of Cornwall. The return journey to London was undertaken by a standard gauge train.

Alfred might have been one of the GWR's lowliest employees working at one of its most obscure stations but he would have known from the day he joined the company that the end of the broad gauge was nigh. Every day of his employment so far he had been able to watch the broad-gauge trains, in his own words, 'roll majestically' through the peaceful Somerset farmland, against the distant backdrop of his own Mendip Hills. Before the opportunity disappeared forever, he wanted to have the joy of travelling on such a train himself. In this section of the memoir, he describes the solitary occasion on which he had that experience.

Alfred would always remember his broad-gauge adventure, not only because of the romance of the train itself but also because it was his first 'grown up' experience of independent travel (although the trip was not without its mundane little annoyances, as we will see).

Three days' leave was the regulation leave allowed to members of the uniform staff in those days and for many years after. One day to get somewhere, one day there, then one day to return. The very first time I was due to this annual holiday with free passes, I had a very exciting, ambitious time of it. My mate did most of the arranging. He was a year older than me and very up to date in his ideas. It was his proposal that we should visit London and Plymouth, travelling on the G.W.R.'s own broad gauge line. We had had the good luck to obtain our leave at the same time. Our combined spending cash was less than £2.

In London we had obtained bed and breakfast at a little side street hotel near Charing Cross Station at 2/6d each and quite all right at that. But this was no chance work, we had been advised to go there by an old seasoned railman. We roamed the streets till the evening then my mate decided we must go to Drury Lane Theatre, more to be able to brag about having been there than for any other reason. Neither of us knew what the play was nor did we trouble to find out – but we'd been to DRURY LANE THEATRE!

Next morning we boarded a broad gauge express at Paddington en route for Plymouth. Such smooth running! One had to look out of a window to be sure the train was moving! We were in one of the finest trains in the world – a G.W.R. broad gauge express bound for the West Country!

Arriving at Plymouth, we were much relieved to get out and stretch our legs for, apart from a short stay at Exeter, we had not left our seats. Our first job was to make sure of obtaining a lodging for the night and we met with a disappointment over this for on enquiry at an address recommended to us, we were told they were full up. We were advised to try at a restaurant a short distance away and there we were successful. Next day we wandered over Plymouth town, went out on the Hoe and climbed to the top of the old Eddystone lighthouse.[20]

Early in the afternoon we had to take train for home and duty. Before leaving for work next morning I showed my old motherly landlady some inflamed patches on my arms – there were others on my body – and asked her if she could tell me the cause. The old lady only grunted but when I came back at dinnertime she handed me a screw of paper saying, 'There's what's been worrying you.' I opened it and saw a nasty looking insect. 'What is it?' says I. 'Why, a bug, that's what 'tis,' said she. That was a souvenir I brought back from Plymouth!

I have always felt pleased since that I made this trip, for in the following year the broad gauge was converted to narrow. A big job quickly done that was – and such strange looking old locomotives came up from the depots in the west. They reminded one of prehistoric monsters come to life. Some of the earliest engines had no cab to protect the enginemen in bad weather!

A broad-gauge engine at Plymouth Millbay Station in 1892. (Great Western Trust)

They and scores of their more modern mates were all making their last journey to the graveyard at Swindon. The works there were quite congested and some were held up for quite a time in the sheds at big depots on the way, places where the mixed gauge was still in use.

There is power in a union

During the last quarter of the nineteenth century, an average of more than 500 railway workers were killed at work each year.[21] Numerous standard working practices, including some of those already described by Alfred, were self-evidently hazardous. Fatigue caused by long working hours was commonplace. Railwaymen's refusal to put up with these working conditions, and the inevitable toll of death and injury that resulted, were the primary reasons for the foundation of the first national railway workers' union, the Amalgamated Society of Railway Servants, in 1872.[22]

By 1900, four more railway unions had been established, each attracting particular occupational groups within the industry. Three of these five unions were eventually to merge to form the National Union of Railwaymen (NUR) in 1913. The membership of the new union at that point was almost 160,000 – a number that demonstrated the extent of recruitment over the preceding decades and indicated the value now placed on the union by railway staff.[23]

Alfred recalls below that he joined the union while still an apprentice at Worle. His decision to do so suggests quite some independence of mind in a lad of only 16 or 17 years old, especially given his situation at a small, out-of-the-way country station that was hardly likely to be a hotbed of demands for better pay and conditions.

As a lad porter I was booked on duty twelve hours a day and I often had to do more. Every other Sunday I had to attend to all the signal lamps as usual and to meet the two or three stopping trains. There was never a ha'penny of overtime or any pay for Sunday duty.

The Railway Union was now beginning to make a stir in some of the big centres.[24] I remember receiving a leaflet inviting employees to attend meetings being held to pass resolutions petitioning for Sunday pay for all grades doing Sunday duty. Some of the more important grades already received it but it was years after before I received any. It was the same with the week-day overtime, for station masters were instructed to book men off duty when they could be spared to balance any overtime they may have worked. Also, men and lads were often shifted to other stations much against their wishes. I had four such shifts in the early years of my service, not through any fault of mine but because it suited the officials.[25] We wanted a trade union in these days, for men were penalised for the least offence and bullied by officials very frequently. For twenty seven years I was a stout advocate of trade unionism.[26]

In what I believe was the earliest strike supported by the union, I was the only member on the station.[27] I was ridiculed and jeered at by my workmates who also prophesised I was certain of the sack later. However, the union gained the terms asked for and there was a return to work for all strikers. My late tormentors 'joined up' almost to a man. I went about with a self-satisfied smile and the jeers of the past week were more like cheers now!

I recall an amusing incident in connection with a later strike. A relief signalman, a nice sociable chap, decided that he would remain loyal to the company although he was almost alone in his decision. After a settlement and a general return to work he was commonly addressed as 'Loyalty' and the name stuck to him. Through defective eyesight he had to acquire spectacles and meeting up with him one day I enquired if he could see better now. 'Oh yes, mate,' said he, 'I see a lot more than I sometimes want to. They forget I get a reflection in these glasses and many of them "make a long nose" at my back after they have passed me by.'[28]

Larking around – and a sudden relocation for Alfred

Although he had already been working full-time for four years, Alfred was still only 16 when he went to work at Worle Station. Despite the long hours that he worked, he still had a 16-year-old's affection for pranks and general larking around. He seems to have made some good friends locally, but in a small village it was necessary to make the very best of whatever limited opportunities for diversion there were; for example, the novelty of the judiciously inserted pin to liven up a church service seems not to have worn off, despite making its first appearance in the memoir when Alfred was still a small boy ...

I was not in the habit of attending chapel services but one Sunday, in company with several lads of about my own age, who had been brought up to chapel, I was induced to go.

We sat in a pew by ourselves and when the sermon started two of the rascals produced pins and inserted them into holes made through the wooden back of the seat in front. These were tiny holes which no-one would notice. They were too small to allow the head of the pin to go through and had a slight upward slope. When the pin was in place, a knee was kept against the head of the pin to operate it. Just a slight push and the point would tickle up the occupant of the seat in front, never very severely, for there was a half inch of wood and the victim's clothes to penetrate before making contact. It was just enough to make a person very fidgety but if he, or she, looked round there was nothing to be seen. Who could attach any suspicion to the youths behind, sitting up so correctly with hands well in sight, proclaiming their innocence? Neat – but hardly reverent. I never attended chapel in their company again.

One autumn evening one of my workmates and I were walking home from the station when we came on a pony feeding on the grass verge. It was harnessed to an empty trap, one wheel of which was right on the edge of a deep rhine. We got the pony out in the road and looked around as well as we could in the dusk to see if there was any trace of humans in or out of the rhine. We found nothing and my mate said, 'Jump up. We'll drive on to the village.' But hardly had we started before two drunken farmers came staggering forward shouting out with many curses for us to stop. They then accused us of driving off their pony and trap and were far too drunk to listen to any explanation. My mate, who held the reins, was threatened with tortures unspeakable but our assailants were too hopelessly incapable to carry out their threats.

We recognised one of them as the owner of the pony and trap and left them to manage as best they could. Next morning, my mate, who was not on duty at the station as early as I was, announced that he was going in to see the belligerent farmer and 'have it out' with him. Later he told me he had settled things all right, and had found farmer a far more reasonable man in the morning than he had been the previous evening. He was generally known as a drunken old rascal and no doubt was glad to hush the matter up.

I nearly came to grief in a rhine one fine summer morning. Our landlady's sailor son, Henry Watts, was home on leave. A fine young man about twenty five years old and he, my mate and I decided to get up early and cut across country to the nearest bit of seaside (about three miles as the crow flies) and have an early morning dip. This we duly did and thoroughly enjoyed it. Returning home, we spied in an adjoining field a grand lot of mushrooms. Over we went and gathered a rare lot, the sailor carrying them in the big towel we had used after bathing. Then on looking round we saw an elderly man on horseback coming through the gateway by which we had entered. Knowing we were trespassing and fearing to lose our haul of mushrooms we started running as hard as we could to the other end of the field.

The horseman was after us calling out, 'Stop! Stop!' but that only urged us on. Then we found ourselves confronted by a deep wide rhine. My two mates who were leading, just cleared it. To me, the youngest, it seemed an impossible leap, but I took it and reached the other side clinging to the bank, feet and legs in the water, scrambled out and off. The old chap on the horse jibbed at the jump and my last glimpse of him was sitting astride his horse brandishing his riding crop and his order was, 'Come back! Now!' Needless to say, we hurried on our way to home and duty – and later enjoyed our mushrooms!

One evening I had to deliver a parcel to a house situated about a half mile outside the village and on the journey, met with one of the biggest scares I ever had. It was getting so dark that one could only see the outlines of things against the sky and there, slowly and menacingly coming towards me, was a most terrifying monster, topped with a pair of conspicuous horns, eight foot up in the air. That satanic nightmare of a thing was only a few yards away now and I was just about paralysed with fear as it came creeping on.

I crouched to the ground and my hand closed on a stone. I was a champion of stone throwing in those days and this stone, about the size of a goose's egg, was just the right weight. The idea flashed in my mind to see what impression a well-aimed piece of rock would have. I rose up and drew back my arm. In another second that stone would have found its target but in the very nick of time the awful horned head was snatched away and disclosed the form of the butcher's assistant who gave a loud guffaw and strode off. He was a man over six feet in height and had killed and skinned a goat and was carrying the skin, head and horns attached, from the slaughterhouse to his home. Being a confirmed joker, when he heard me coming he could not resist having his bit of fun.

I reckon he didn't realise what an appalling sight he was when decked out in that skin topped by the significant horns. He would have loved to have been able to brag how he'd made the porter from the station run away shouting with fright – but he didn't quite manage it. Near thing, though. But for that handy stone I guess he'd have won. I've often thought since it was a pity the stone was not hurled as long as he was not seriously hurt by it!

I made a close friend of a young man of seventeen who had obtained a situation as van man at the laundry. Quite a big place that laundry.[29] It employed all the women who wanted work for a mile or two around and quite a few men. Will Came[30] was my friend's name and he was one of the best, modest and truthful, with a rare talent for music – so much so that a lady in his native village had him trained and even when a schoolboy he played the church organ.

As an employee at the laundry Will possessed a key to the premises and he proposed, one Sunday morning, that we should enter and have a hot bath. I readily agreed. There was abundance of hot water in the big boilers and filling two large tubs we revelled in a good long soak, such as I had not enjoyed for many a long day. Many times after we took similar liberties on the laundry company's premises, and very enjoyable they were. Country folk didn't do much bathing in those days. Saturday nights, in most respectable families, the nippers were 'tubbed' but for most grownups, bath nights were few and far between.

As another winter approached, we lads hardly knew how to spend the long evenings. There was no reading room in the village, although such places were being provided in many more progressive villages. A retired army officer very kindly allowed books to be borrowed from his large library at certain times on certain days – but that was of little use to us.

Then one day, Will happened to hear that the village once boasted of a fife and drum band and that the instruments were still in the care of the parson. Will and I took the very first chance that we had to wait on His Reverence and, bless him, he at once agreed to our taking over the instruments and said he would arrange for us to have the lighted schoolroom to practice in. We were well away, and at once enlisted four more lads all of whom would get a few notes from a fife.

When we met for first practice Will was unanimously hailed as bandmaster and he proposed that we at once start learning to play carols, so that we should be ready at Christmas to tour the neighbourhood and rake in the shekels. We all heartily agreed and under Will's tuition went at it most earnestly – no printed music and no drummers yet. We were all determined to memorise the old, well-known carols and, before we parted that night, we could all toot out 'While Shepherds Watched'. Of course, you mustn't be finicky over a few false notes!

Alas! all my hopes of pleasant evenings were washed out the very next morning for Station Master said he had notice from Head Office that I was to report to Bristol next day for duty there. I met Will that same evening and he suggested that we should both join the army. I did not fancy a soldier's life but agreed to try for the navy if he would but Will did not want to be a sailor, so we each decided to go his own way. Soon after I left, Will did enlist and he wrote later that he was in the regimental band playing a clarinet. A few months later he was sent on a draft to India and wrote me many interesting letters from there.

Settling in the 'great city'

No explanation is given for Alfred's sudden posting to Bristol but it seems at least possible that a spell at Temple Meads Station, the spiritual home of the GWR, was part of the training for all uniformed staff. The difficulty for Alfred – as we have already seen – is that he is not at all enamoured of Bristol. He had previously found it unsettling, perhaps even rather threatening, with its constant noise and its apparent chaos. This is not surprising. More than anything else, perhaps, Alfred's memoir reveals him as a country lad, made happy by the quiet lanes and stone cottages of his home village and the constancy of family and friends. In the physically similar surroundings of Worle, he had found this solid, cheerful life easy to replicate. Bristol was to be a challenge.

My new job and city life were so unpleasant to me that at the end of the first week I was on the verge of leaving the company's service. Things were not very comfortable in my lodgings either. This was no fault of the landlady. She was a good soul but there were three children all under school age and between caring for them and her husband, the lodger got scant attention. Then an old schoolmate working in a hat factory in Bristol who had obtained my address from home called for me and every evening after that we went out seeking adventure.

My friend owned a high 'penny-farthing' bicycle. The 'safety cycle'[31] was just getting popular and I hired one for sixpence an hour from a cycle shop. With my mate's aid I learned to ride it. This was quite an accomplishment in those days. But of course I couldn't spend sixpences on hire of a machine very often, so sometimes my mate rode off alone. One evening he ran over a cat and was so injured by the fall he had from the high seat of his bike that he had to have a long spell in hospital. He then had to have time at home to recover his strength. He found other employment and never returned to Bristol but I'd got hardened now and determined to stick it.

I now had a weekly wage of twelve shillings but had to pay ten shillings for board and lodging. There was two shillings left to provide myself with clothes, boots and any amusement I fancied. Every morning between 10.00 and 11.00, a push barrow fitted with a charcoal fire and loaded with cakes and buns was to be met with near the station and I just couldn't resist the temptation of having a ha'penny cup of hot coffee and a ha'penny pancake. That meant one sixth of my two shillings gone west.

My finances did not allow me to visit theatres or any such places. Cinemas were not yet in existence. I took out books from a big public library situated near Trinity Church but had very little comfort to sit down and read them. But I was buoyed up by the knowledge that I should be shifted when I attained eighteen years of age to – I hoped – more congenial company and conditions.

My lodgings were situated in a quiet side street on Barton Hill, good class houses but ours proved not to be weatherproof. We had a real blizzard one day that winter, followed by a quick thaw. As I prepared to get into bed I found the coverlet was wet and called the landlord up, for water was coming from the ceiling. We shifted the bed to a drier spot and placed a bath under the leak. We waited about a half hour but the flow had slightly increased instead of stopping and we were afraid to go to bed in case the bath overflowed. There was no trapdoor to give access to the upper regions and my landlord decided to help matters by driving the poker up through the ceiling. This produced a steady flow about the size of a man's finger. The bath was soon filled and we had to carry buckets full downstairs and ended up by throwing the water out of the window to the yard below.

It seemed that all the snow which had penetrated through the roofs of all that row of houses had gravitated to the space over my bedroom ceiling. It would have been a rare flood in the house if the early drip had not been discovered.

As a country-bred boy there was never any mistaking the homestead door but when I first went to this town lodging, several times in the summer when the street doors were open, I barged my way into a neighbour's house in mistake. If I met no-one and saw unfamiliar bits of furniture, I quickly backed out but once or twice had to apologise.

'You get used to it' – working life in Bristol

I soon started to learn what hard dirty work was. My duties consisted mostly in dealing with scores of signal lamps perched on the tops of high posts amid the complicated mass of lines and sidings which were laid out there. What a drastic change from the little country station I had left, where the surroundings were so pleasant. My signals began about a quarter mile outside the main station and extended to the outskirts where there were tanneries, horse slaughterers' yards, sugar refineries and large manure works – a combination which created such a stench that it appalled a country bred lad. But as an old worker remarked, 'You get used to it.'

We had another severe winter when I was a lamp-lad in Bristol and well I knew it. Having to climb those iron ladders when they were all coated with frost, a fresh one every few yards, was a real hardship. Unless one moved quickly one's hands would just stick to the iron. I spent a couple of my rare shillings on a pair of leather gloves but they proved about useless for after one or two trips up the ladders they became so slippery that it was difficult to retain a grip with them and many times I came near having about a thirty foot fall.

One near scrape I'm never likely to forget. I was on the end of the little platform on top of a signal post with a couple of lamps in one hand when my feet slipped from under me and I was hanging by one hand from the iron guard rail. Down went the lamps to be smashed up on the rails below and I had to kick and struggle to reach a foot out as far as possible to hitch it on to the ladder and then by wriggling along I managed to regain safety. It was a near call and as it happened, there was nobody near enough just then to give a bit of assistance.

I was shocked one morning when I called at one of the biggest signal cabins in Bristol to collect the 'train delay sheets', to see the lad telegraphist crying copiously. He was a beginner of about fourteen years of age and because he could not quite keep up to the work, that rascal of a signalman was violently abusing him. A facility to 'send' was soon acquired but it was much harder to 'read' for most messages came from a big office staffed by experts and they just would not send slowly to give a tyro the chance to spell it out.

In spite of my portrayal of this bully of a signalman though, I reckon the old signalmen of those days were a fine lot of men. In the early days of railways they were styled as policemen and one old chap I knew kept a staff in his signal-box – for in his young days he was equipped with a top hat and staff. He was now entitled to wear thirteen stripes on his tunic sleeve – one stripe for every four years of efficient service. As a youngster, I was on friendly terms with a local preacher, a teacher of the violin, a Salvation Army bandmaster, a professional bass singer and other worthies who drew their weekly wages as signalmen.

The area surrounding Bristol Temple Meads Station. This photograph was taken a decade or two after Alfred worked there but the general impression – a 'complicated mass of lines and sidings' – is unchanged. (STEAM – Museum of the GWR, Swindon)

A signal box (or cabin) was strictly forbidden ground to any of the public and even to all other railwaymen unless they had a business reason to be there. A signalman must always show himself at a window and watch passing trains. This was a very necessary procedure and many accidents were prevented by his taking prompt action.

When on duty the signalman must always be in uniform, even to wearing his uniform cap – but so many neglected this last order that it was amended to uniform cap or none. Like all the other uniform staff he was never supposed to smoke when on duty. Most of them had plenty of chance to indulge in tobacco though, shut up for a twelve-hour spell of duty all on their own, except for a chance visit by an official.

I was up in one of the big junction signal boxes one afternoon and as the booking lad and I were looking out of a window, we saw a man fall from a twenty foot high wall down on the line about a hundred yards distant. The signalman threw his signals to 'Danger' against an approaching train and immediately sent us two lads off to see if the man was clear of the rails. The checked train came to a stop right on the scene of the accident before we reached there and to our relief, the guard, assisted by several passengers, hoisted the unconscious man into his van and he was carried off into Temple Meads Station and from there to hospital.

When I left the depot that evening there was a girl about nine years of age standing in the light of the gate lamp. She held a shawl up to her body and as I was passing said 'Please sir ('sir' – to me!), can you tell me what they have done with the man who fell over the wall?' I replied, 'He's been taken to hospital. Why?' 'He was my father,' she said, with sobs and tears. 'Where is your mother?' I asked. 'Gone to find father,' she sobbed and as she spoke she opened her shawl to get a fresh grip on something inside it and I just caught sight of an almost naked baby. Then she whimpered, 'I'm so hungry,' and I quite believed her.

It was near the end of the week and I only possessed fourpence but I gave her tuppence. She appeared most grateful and as I said 'Goodnight,' she hurried off and I feel sure that twopence was exchanged for a bit of food as quickly as ever she could reach a suitable shop.

I never saw the girl again but I heard that her father was a ne'er do well and was half drunk when he climbed over the railway boundary wall and fell on the

A GWR 'lamp boy'. This photograph is believed to have been taken in the early twentieth century rather than the late nineteenth, but it gives a good sense of the working life of the young lad responsible for making sure the lamps were where they should be and in proper working order. (STEAM – Museum of the GWR, Swindon)

line far below. He had a long enforced stay in hospital and I hope it reformed him. Many a time since I've wished I had given that forlorn, hungry little girl my whole fortune of fourpence. I've felt satisfaction at the recollection of the twopence I did part with, and would dearly like it to have been doubled.

There were many women and children going about hungry then. Unemployment and consequent poverty was rife amongst the working classes that winter and when a working man did have a shilling or two in his pocket it was a common practice to take it to the public house. In midwinter, boys seven to twelve years of age with no boots or socks on their feet would be on the streets and going inside public houses trying to sell evening papers. They would be blue with the cold but the publican prospered and a man who couldn't drink up several pints of beer at a sitting was regarded as a weakling in many working class quarters.

My lamp-room at Bristol was situated right close to the carriage sidings and I at once became acquainted with 'Tiny', such smart little engine as was ever turned out of the works. I said to the fireman, 'What a pretty little engine.' 'Yes,' said he. 'That's our Tiny.' She was engaged in hauling carriages in and out of Temple Meads Station. There may have been others like her but I have never seen one before or since. Quite small – when she was pushing a long row of coaches you wondered what was moving them, for you couldn't see Tiny until she came up abreast of you. Lots of brass about her, including a big brass bell and it was always kept as bright as human hands could keep it

For months I was seeing Tiny quite a lot and came to know that her driver and fireman made quite an idol of her. Then one day a sad-looking fireman told me, 'We're losing Tiny.' 'How's that?' I enquired. 'She had to be sent to Swindon,' said he. 'Oh, but you'll get her back, won't you?' I queried. ''fraid not. They once get her up there they'll keep her.' A day or two afterwards Tiny was gone and the coaches were being worked by a common looking 'side tank' engine and a dejected looking driver and fireman.

Broad-gauge graveyard

One day, I went into an old engine shed and there, to my great surprise, were several of the grand old broad gauge 'fliers'. 'Swallow' was one and I climbed

Scores of redundant broad-gauge locomotives await scrapping in Swindon in 1892. (Great Western Trust)

up on the footplate and grasping the regulator, pretended to start her up.[32] Her fire had been out for weeks and she would never move under her own steam again, so I said 'goodbye' to the old lady who had been the pride of her driver for years and was now awaiting her doom.

It seemed so wicked to scrap those grand engines. All the major battles of the Crimean war were commemorated in their names – 'Sebastapol', 'Inkermann', 'Balaclava', 'Alma' and so on. Others which occur to me are 'Tornado', 'Lightning', 'Cyclone', 'Swallow' and of course 'Lord of the Isles'.

The brass letters composing the names and arranged in an arch over the driving wheels were always so clean and bright that anyone with average sight could read them at twenty yards' distance. The paintwork always looked fresh and was often gone over with cotton waste and tallow by the fireman, who would sometimes finish off with a series of wavy lines running along the length of the boiler. After the conversion to the narrow gauge and the consequent destruction of these world famous engines many influential men obtained the names in brass letters and had them mounted on polished wood in an arch, as they had originally appeared over the engine wheels.

Sometime later, the name from 'Inkermann' was brought by a gentleman to the country station where I was working and I had the honour of helping place it in his carriage when he took it away to his residence, to be placed over one of his doorways. What a change for 'Inkermann' after being rushed through towns and villages all over the west country to be fixed irremovably in a quiet country house.

Although the conditions of employment in those days were very hard, most employees were proud to serve the G.W.R. and were very jealous of the company's reputation.[33] Not a railway man in the west, from lamp-lad to superintendent but knew the 'Flying Dutchman'. I doubt if any other train, before or since, ever made such an appeal to the public. It was a real treat to anyone interested in railways to see her rolling along so stately and smoothly on her daily journey – Paddington to Plymouth and vice versa.[34]

Later in my career, I would be thrilled by a sight of the 'Great Bear', the heaviest loco of her time.[35] She would take eighty loaded wagons or a hundred empties but had a short life, I heard, for the reason that she was too heavy for the permanent way as it was in those days. Moreover, such a train as she pulled could not be accommodated at many stations, so just had to have a clear run through and this was not always convenient.

I also remember what admiration the 'Castles' created when first put on the road. A tale was that when the G.W.R. and another trunk line exchanged locos for experiment our Great Western man was looking round his engine preparatory to a start when an official told him they were putting on a vehicle over the usual load. The driver pointed with pride to his massive machine and said 'Put as many more as you like, she'll take 'em' – and so she did and won great credit.[36]

A great fire in Bristol

On Saturday 14 May 1892, a massive and terrifying fire at the warehouses of the Bear Creek Oil and Shipping Company, situated at Temple Back, destroyed 200ft of frontage onto the River Avon near to Temple Meads Station.

Broad-gauge locomotive *Swallow*, whose footplate Alfred climbed aboard at Bristol after she was de-commissioned in 1892. (Great Western Trust)

The warehouses contained thousands of barrels of petrol, seal oil and colza oil. The extent of the fire was so great that it spread to the surface of the river on floating oil and travelled to the opposite bank where a distillery caught fire. Under the banner headline, 'Disastrous Fire at Bristol – The Avon Ablaze' the *Pall Mall Gazette* of 16 May reported that several floating vessels were consumed by flaming oil, including five barges and a dredger. This looks certain to have been the fire that Alfred witnessed and recorded in his memoir.

One fine afternoon the sun, in our quarter of Bristol, was suddenly obscured by dense clouds of smoke coming over from the direction of Temple Meads. Every employee who could possibly leave his job ran off to see if the station was on fire but we found that the thick black clouds of smoke were coming from a big oil and colour factory situated close to the goods yard at Temple Meads with just the river in between.

It was near high tide and oil was floating all over the water. At times the flames would roar up and over the river, last for a few minutes, then die down to be repeated as more oil came from the burning factory. In one of the lulls between the flames, a rowing boat containing three men came on the scene. The men got out of the boat to examine the walls of the factory which were only a foot or two from the water. Two men re-entered the boat but by some mischance the third man stumbled and over went the boat and all three men went in and under the water.

There were a few tense moments with not a sound from the many onlookers, then three heads appeared puffing and blowing. It was soon apparent that all three men could swim. Then there was much laughter for they were fat middle-aged men fully clothed and they puffed and spluttered a good deal as they swam the few yards to our side and safety. I was wondering what would happen to them if the flames had chanced to come roaring long just then. I never heard but that they got over their immersion all right but if they had swallowed only one mouthful of that filthy water one would have expected a stomach pump to be necessary.

Alfred turns 18 and cycles off into the future

Alfred ends his memoir by reporting an apparently inconsequential event – his purchase of a second-hand bicycle. At this distance in time, though, it is easy to forget the sense of cutting-edge modernity associated with cycling at this time. In 1892 when Alfred bought his bike, the engineering improvements associated with the safety bicycle had just begun to hint at the full potential of cycling, which had previously appeared suitable only for the eccentric and the foolhardy.[37] After all, there had been no other advance in rider-operated personal transport since humans first began to ride horses several millennia earlier.

Early bike owners must have felt a huge sense of personal freedom and there was considerable social cachet too. Most early cyclists were drawn from the better-off groups in society and were generally regarded as rather sporting. For Alfred and other working-class cyclists, there must also have been the feeling that owning a bike was a real indicator of getting on in the world. Most of these pioneering early cyclists joined clubs in order to meet other enthusiasts, and the fact that some adventurous young women took up the activity added a pleasing element of raciness to the thing. The amount of cash required was daunting though. Alfred's bike cost him £3 – exactly five weeks' wages – perhaps the equivalent of over £1,000 at current prices.

One day I heard of a bicycle for sale at a private house and, in the company of a cycling friend, went to inspect it. Three pounds was the price asked and we decided it was a bargain. I had not been able to save up 3 shillings, much less £3 but in my page boy days I had given all I earned, or received, to my mother and she would put it in the Post Office Savings Bank for me. There was £5 to my credit there. Now, in a spirit of recklessness, I arranged to draw out £3 to buy that second-hand bike.

What a museum piece it would look today! All metal parts except the chain painted black, solid red rubber tyres about the thickness of a man's finger and a massive chain — but it worked, and I was very proud of it. As a recruit of the Richmond Cycling Club and only a few days after I possessed it, I rode it to Clevedon and back — about twenty four miles — quite an exploit in those days.

Previous to the next Sunday when I was free, I wrote home to say I should be cycling out to them on the Saturday evening. A mile from home I met with quite an ovation, for my brother, accompanied by several old schoolmates, had walked out that far to meet me. None of them could ride but there was quite a squabble as to who should have the honour of wheeling my bike. It was the only one in the village.

I was glad enough to walk for, although I had been on a main road all the way, it was far more bumpy than any minor road today. There would always be lengths of freshly laid stones, over which riding was impossible. Nothing for it but to dismount and walk! My father examined my bike with an amused smile and when I invited him to have a go on it, he shook his head and said, 'Sooner have a horse.' I had fine weather for my journey both ways and was back in Bristol on duty at 7.00 a.m. on the Monday morning. I rode that old solid-tyred bike for about two years then sold it for the same price I had paid — £3.

Soon I reached eighteen years of age, when G.W.R. employees were either kept on as men or discharged. I was kept on. The very day I reached eighteen I was sent off to a country station with a wage of fifteen shillings a week. I was properly 'in the money' now.[38] I was very glad to leave town and enjoy the sweet country-air again. I was also happy to find as time went on that, once again, the station master was a man anyone might be proud to work under. A good, honest God-fearing man he was.

But as this yarn is intended only to deal with my youth I must now say 'Goodbye' for I have reached manhood as laid down in the Great Western Railway Rules and Regulations.

EPILOGUE

The first time I read Alfred Plumley's memoir it was the 'social history' aspect of it that caught my attention. The memoir was interesting because it revealed details about rural life and the day-to-day working world of the railways that I could not have found from any other source. I thought that it deserved a wider readership because I could see that other people would find these insights interesting too. That is still the case — and I hope you have enjoyed this element of the book — but, of course, the first time I read it, the memoir was completely anonymous. I had no idea even of Alfred's name let alone the names of any the people he wrote about. I didn't know the location of any of the events that he described either, apart from the general fact that they took place in Somerset.

As I did my research and began to slot the real names of people and places into the memoir, I began to understand that there was also a human dimension to Alfred's story. A name is a simple thing but it has a disproportionate effect in bestowing substance. Give a place its real name and it magically becomes so substantial that you can actually look it up on a map, hop in the car and visit it. It may have changed a bit since the late nineteenth century but you can walk around it and 130-year-old events will appear before your eyes. You can't visit a person from the nineteenth century so easily, but the principle is pretty much the same. Give that person a name and even though they are long dead, they will begin somehow to assume shape and personality, flitting between tangibility and intangibility like a genie conjured from a lamp. As I read and re-read the memoir I began to see and hear the young Alfred in my mind. I wouldn't go so far as to say that he felt like someone I actually knew. It was more as if, by some strange shift in history, he had become an actual ancestor of mine – one of my great-grandfathers maybe – just by virtue of my having stumbled upon his story on that cold afternoon two years before.

Alfred married in 1899. He and his wife Kate had three daughters and a son, all born before 1910. Alfred's son died while still a young, single man but Alfred's three daughters all married and had children (in fact, they all married on the same day in 1930 in a triple wedding ceremony). It is possible that Alfred's great-grandchildren and great-great-grandchildren do not even know his name; it is the fate of most of us to be forgotten after a couple of generations and the same is likely be true of Alfred. His photograph may still exist in a shoebox in an attic somewhere, but if it does it is likely that the person who one day finds it will scratch their head and wonder just who this chap is.

It was a photograph of Alfred that I hoped for most of all when I visited the archive of the Museum of the Great Western Railway in Swindon to look for illustrations for this book. I thought it just possible that the archive might hold a staff group photograph, taken long ago at some West Country station or another, on which Alfred appeared, seated on a bench smiling alongside his fellow porters, ticket collectors and booking clerks, all dressed in their best uniforms. Or, maybe, in a back copy of the GWR staff magazine there would

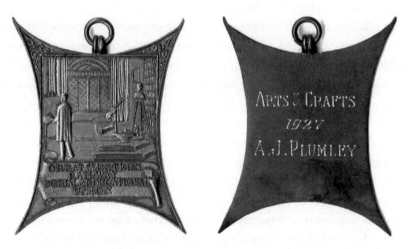

Alfred's 1927 medal for woodcarving. (STEAM – Museum of the GWR, Swindon)

be a little biography of Alfred with a picture of him at the top, published, say, to note a significant promotion or maybe on the occasion of his retirement after forty-five years' loyal service. It was not to be. I walked back to the station to catch the train home, pleased with the other photographs found but disappointed that Alfred had remained elusive.

Then, three weeks later, my phone rang. It was the assistant curator in Swindon who had helped me with my search. An odd thing had happened. In order to answer an entirely unrelated enquiry, she had, the previous day, had to search through some of the large number of small artefacts held in storage at the archive. Mostly these types of items have been donated to the museum by ex-GWR employees and their descendants or have been given by collectors. Among the items was a small bronze medal. It was not relevant to the enquiry the assistant curator was answering and she was just about to replace it in its box when she noticed the engraved name of the recipient – 'A.J. Plumley'.

I can therefore tell you that, in 1927, Alfred won third prize in 'Class 8: Woodcarving' of the annual arts and crafts competition held by the GWR Social and Educational Union. Of course, this is an absurdly tiny detail to know about Alfred's later life but it is neatly in keeping with the modest nature of the events recorded in the memoir. It is nice also to look at the medal (shown opposite) and know that one day in 1927 Alfred turned it over in his hands. I imagine he was pleased to receive it, even though he would presumably have preferred gold or silver. According to the results of the competition announced in the *Great Western Railway Magazine*, those medals went, respectively, to H.J. Gazard of Wormwood Scrubs Station and another Alfred, Alfred E. Evans, at Paddington. But then again, H.J. Gazard and Alfred E. Evans have not had their memoirs published.

The museum's catalogue showed that a magazine cutting had been donated along with the medal. This cutting, when retrieved, turned out to be a very short article about Alfred and his woodcarving hobby, trimmed from an unknown publication – perhaps a local-interest magazine or a specialist journal for woodworkers.

The article reported that Alfred favoured the traditional carving technique known as 'chip carving'. This piece of information unexpectedly cleared up the mystery of Alfred's original choice of title for his memoir, *Chip of the*

The mantlepiece of Alfred's home in Chippenham, Wiltshire, sometime around 1927. (STEAM – Museum of the GWR, Swindon)

Mendips (mentioned, if you remember, in the introductory section of this book). More pleasingly still, the article was illustrated with a photograph of some of the items carved by Alfred, on display on the mantlepiece of the Plumley family home in Chippenham in Wiltshire. The photograph (reproduced above) shows a carved and fretworked clock-case and various other decorative objects. One of these objects hanging on the wall is a carved photograph frame. Look carefully and you will see that the frame contains a photograph. It is just about possible to make out a man standing with his arm around a woman seated in a chair. This must surely be Alfred with Kate. So there was a photograph after all, but just a very small one that had almost been lost. Just a little detail in a larger picture. Like the memoir itself, a glimpse.

Notes

Alfred Plumley: Family and Circumstances, 1879

1. The website *Measuring Worth* (www.measuringworth.com) is an academic resource that uses historical data to make accurate comparisons of monetary values between different historical periods. The site's 'Labour Value' calculator suggests that Freddy's weekly wage of 18s is equivalent to around £400 at 2016 values. Elsewhere in the memoir, Alfred tells us that the usual wage for an agricultural labourer at that time was between 9 and 12s a week. This is equivalent to around £200–£270 in 2016. Only the upper end of this range is at the level of today's national minimum wage, so it is easy to see that most Mendip villagers were likely to be poor. The Plumley family, although on what was still a modest income, would nevertheless have been comfortably off by comparison with many of their neighbours, especially as they also had the benefit of rent-free accommodation.

1. Schoolboy

1. See note 1 to Family and Circumstances, 1879. Threepence per child per week, the amount paid by Alfred's parents for Alfred and Edward to go to school, was $\frac{1}{72}$ part of Freddy's weekly wage. This is roughly equivalent to around £5.50 at present-day prices, a sum which was presumably within Freddy's reach but would perhaps have been a lot more difficult to find for many other village families.

2.   The traditional manual method for separating edible grain from the non-edible husks and stalk – the chaff – involved farm labourers repeatedly beating heaps of harvested cereal crops with a flail. The flail was made of two lengths of wood hinged at the centre, one part forming a handle, the other being used to strike the grain. This process usually happened on a special, flat 'threshing floor', generally inside a barn or shed. It was tough, time-consuming, physical work, requiring a number of men. By 1880, as Alfred observes, the manual process had been superseded in many places by the use of a steam-operated threshing machine. Whether the threshing was done by hand or by machine, the resultant material was then winnowed to further refine the grain. Sometimes this involved just allowing the wind to blow through the grain. Alfred describes the workers in this case using a winnowing machine – a hand-cranked device that allowed the grain to fall through a grid into a container while the finer chaff would blow away.

3.   'Tommy' was originally an eighteenth-century military slang term for bread. The word gradually came into general use as a term for a working man's daily provisions, hence 'tommy bag' for the bag in which the food was carried. Partridge, E., *Slang, Today and Yesterday* (London: Routledge, 1933).

4.   It is curious that Alfred's memories of his schooldays include only boys. Burrington School was a mixed school. Perhaps, in this instance, he was only sent to the homes of absent boys and a female pupil had the same responsibility for visiting absent girls.

5.   'Catty' and 'Duckey' have evaded research and must remain unexplained but 'Warney' was evidently a form of 'tag' or 'tick'. In this variation, the single child who started the game off had to chase the other players. As soon as he tagged one of the others, that player would have to join hands with him. These two would then chase the others together until another child was tagged and that player would then have to join hands with the first two. The game proceeded in this way until every child but one was holding hands. The last remaining child was the winner. (Precisely this same game was rather unimaginatively called 'chain tick' in my primary school in

the 1960s.) Gomme, A.B., *The Traditional Children's Games of England, Scotland & Ireland in Dictionary Form, Volume II* (London: David Nutt, 1898).

6.   The other three games will be familiar to most people, at least by name, but 'Truckle the Trencher' is surely lost in the mists of time. The description of the game below is from 'Dorsetshire Children's Games', an article in Volume 7 of *The Folk-Lore Journal* published in 1889:

> This used to be a standard game for winter evenings. A circle was formed, and each one was seated on the floor, every player taking the name of a flower. One player stood in the midst and commenced to spin the trencher round on the floor as fast as possible, at the same time calling for one of the flowers represented by the other players seated in the ring. The bearer of the name had to rush forward and seize the trencher before it fell to the ground, or else pay a forfeit, which was redeemed in the usual manner at the close of the game. This game was entered into with the greatest vivacity by staid and portly individuals as well as by their juniors.

It is interesting that the game was identified by *The Folk-Lore Journal* as belonging to Somerset's neighbouring county of Dorset. It was perhaps particular to the region.

7.   The *Oxford English Dictionary* (*OED*) gives 'dominie' as a specifically Scottish word for a schoolmaster, rooted in the Latin term *dominus* (master). The term had been in common use in Scotland for several centuries where it had long been the policy of the Church of Scotland to try to provide a schoolmaster in every community (the church minister often fulfilling both roles). It seems an unlikely term for Alfred to use at the opposite end of Great Britain. Perhaps Schoolmaster could have been a Scot who introduced the term 'dominie' to his pupils.

8.   Primrose ointment was an established folk remedy for the treatment of wounds, although it seems more usually to have been the leaves rather than the heads of the flower that were used. Kemsey's

The British herbal; or, a practical treatise on the uses and application of the common herbs of Great Britain (Bristol: published by the author, 1838) suggests that 'a fine salve for green wounds [fresh wounds] may be made from the leaves of the primrose'. Typically, the primroses were crushed into butter or lard and simmered for a while before the resultant mixture was decanted into jars where it would set. *Lotions and Potions: Recipes of Women's Institute Members and their Ancestors,* edited by Gwynedd Lloyd (London: Federation of Women's Institutes, 1965), suggests it is the residue left in the strainer after primrose ointment has been made that is 'useful to cure bad cuts'. This residue presumably contains the petals.

9. The Drawbridge, as Alfred says, was a bridge with a lifting mechanism to allow tall ships to pass into the docks. It was situated in the centre of Bristol at Clare Street (now Baldwin Street). It was replaced with a new fixed bridge, St Augustine's Bridge, in 1893. The old bridge had evidently become notorious for causing the traffic to snarl up, which is precisely the experience of it that Alfred and his father seem to have had.

10. At the time of Alfred's memoir, Westbury-on-Trym was still a separate village in Gloucestershire, about 3 miles north of Bristol. It has since been absorbed by the expansion of the city and is now a suburb.

11. Alfred describes a 'dilly' in detail later in the text. The *OED* defines the word as local to Somerset, referring to it as 'a light platform cart', 'a frame on wheels for carrying teazles' and 'a low four-wheeled truck'.

12. Unless otherwise indicated, all of the detail about the teasel trade in these paragraphs is taken from the comprehensive study *Teazles and Teazlemen: The teazle trade in the West Riding of Yorkshire since the eighteenth century* by Robert A. McMillan (privately published in book form and online at www.teazlesandteazlemen.co.uk). I also acknowledge, with thanks, the further information kindly supplied by Robert in personal correspondence.

13. *Penny Magazine,* 30 September 1840.

14. A nineteenth-century trade journal advertisement for William North & Son, Teazle Merchants of Leeds, shows a small cart laden with packs of teasels to almost four times the height of a man.

15. Charles Plumley died in the early autumn of 1886 when Alfred was aged 12.

16. In 1829 it was noted that teasels 'cannot be stacked like corn, as pressure destroys the spine and a free circulation of air is required to dry them thoroughly. Barns, sheds and even the very bedrooms of the cottages are crowded with them'. Knapp, J.L., *The Journal of a Naturalist* (London: J. Murray, 1829).

17. Knapp (note 17, above) also noted that, depending on whether the season was a good or bad one, teasels were 'a source of rapid wealth to some, and injury to others – teazles are emphatically called a "casualty crop"'.

18. A sheep's head clock is a particular form of brass lantern clock that has a larger dial than other forms. Typically, lantern clocks were wall-mounted and had a weight-driven, thirty-hour movement. They did not keep time particularly accurately and had only one hand. Minutes were gauged by the position of the hour hand on the dial. Lantern clocks were the most common type of domestic clock from the mid seventeenth century onwards but were already pretty much obsolete by the time of Charles Plumley's death.

19. This unfortunate little boy seems almost certain to have been the son of the Plumleys' nearest neighbours, Henry and Jane Baber. Henry Baber's occupation is given in the 1881 census as 'bootmaker'. Henry's finding among the smoking embers as the only intact remnant of the boy's short life – the shoe he had himself made just a few weeks before – gives this tragic story something of the qualities of a fable. It is not surprising that Alfred can recall the incident in so much detail.

20. Most likely the Third Voluntary Battalion of the Somerset Light Infantry. Langford History Group, *Every House Tells a Story* (Langford: Langford History Group, 2006).

21. Both voluntary and board schools often suffered from limited teaching capacity. In the earlier nineteenth century, many schools supplemented their teaching staff by using 'monitors' – more able older pupils – to provide instruction for the younger children. In

the late 1840s, the role of monitor was formalised into a five-year paid apprenticeship as 'pupil-teacher'. Alfred tells us on more than one occasion that his brother Edward was a bright boy and it is not surprising to hear that he became a pupil-teacher. More noteworthy is that at the end of his apprenticeship Edward won a Queen's Scholarship to attend teacher-training college. A limited number of these scholarships was available nationally, and to win one was a significant achievement for a lad from Edward's background. Edward went on to become a teacher.

22.   Whortleberry, known as bilberry in the north of England and braeberry in Scotland, occurs naturally only on heathland and moorland. The bushes grow low to the ground and can be quite difficult to spot. Because of this low-growing habit, the berries are hard work to pick. The whortleberry plant has defied attempts at cultivation and in former times was regarded by working people as a rare delicacy. Whortleberries were generally baked in pies or used to make jam.

23.   It is hard to imagine a more peremptory assertion of privilege than the one described in this incident. In this moment, Alfred's family seem to have lost an asset that, at least potentially, might have been worth a significant sum of money to the family at a later date. The 'Lord of the Manor' is not named but seems most likely to have been the Fourth Duke of Cleveland (1803–92). The duke owned almost 100,000 acres in nine counties from Cornwall to Durham. His relatively modest holdings of 5,000 acres in Somerset included Wrington Manor, which encompassed much of the open land around Burrington and Langford. The duke himself lived between his homes at Raby Castle in County Durham, Battle Abbey in Sussex and his house in London. He is reported seldom to have visited the manor of Wrington, so possibly the story of Freddy's little parcel of land had become exaggerated in the telling and the man he actually encountered that day was the duke's agent or bailiff, rather than the duke himself. 'Obituary of the Duke of Cleveland', *Northern Echo*, 22 August 1892; Dunning, R., *Victorian and Edwardian Somerset* (Stroud: Amberley Books, 2008).

24. 'Gruff hole' is a dialect phrase specific to Somerset. It refers to a shallow trench or depression excavated for the purposes of extracting minerals or ore. A man who worked a gruff hole was known as a 'gruffer'. Williams, W.P. and Jones, W.A., *A Glossary of Provincial Words & Phrases in use in Somersetshire.* (London: Longmans, Green, Reader and Dyer, 1873).

25. 'Gold crested wren' is an archaic term for the bird now known simply as the goldcrest.

26. Like his son-in-law, Thomas Somers was also a Justice of the Peace.

27. 'A study of Velvet Bottom and its dams, Charterhouse on Mendip', Charterhouse Environs Research Team (CHERT: 2009). Retrieved from www.chert.org.uk.

28. *Western Times*, 5 January 1914.

29. Maggs, C.G., *The Branch Lines of Somerset* (Stroud: Amberley Books, 2009).

30. The lads from HMS *Formidable* were not naval cadets as one might imagine (and as Alfred may have believed). In the second half of the nineteenth century, a number of redundant naval vessels were leased to local charitable bodies in port cities for use either as homes for orphan boys; reformatory institutions for homeless boys convicted of minor offences; or industrial schools where poor boys might learn a trade. HMS *Formidable*, anchored at Portishead in Bristol and renamed the National Nautical School, was one such vessel. Its inmates were destitute boys from Bristol who had appeared before the magistrates. Typically the boys sent to live on these ex-naval vessels were aged between 10 and 15. Discipline was often extremely harsh but within the context of the times, the intention was benevolent. The idea was to turn out boys suited to a life in the Royal Navy or the merchant services, or to equip them for life as solid, law-abiding adult citizens in some other way. Many of the institutions taught musical skills and formed a band from the inmates. I am grateful to Peter Higginbotham's research for this information (see note 32, below).

31. All the information about Axbridge Workhouse in these paragraphs comes from the comprehensive web resource

www.workhouses.org.uk, maintained and researched by
Peter Higginbotham.

32. The caption beneath an 1886 engraving of Evan Henry Llewellyn
in the *Illustrated London News* describes him as 'Deputy Lieutenant of
Somerset and Chairman of the Axbridge Board of Guardians'.

2. Alfred Plumley: Servant

1. '5th Standard' refers to a measure of educational attainment in the
Revised Code of 1862, which was introduced by the National
Committee of Council on Education. It was a form of payment
by results, which stipulated that the grant payments paid by central
government to individual schools would be calculated by reference
to the numbers of children in that school who had achieved one of
six educational 'standards'. These standards roughly corresponded to
the expected level of intelligence for each age group between 7 and
12 (Standard 1 for 7-year-olds, Standard 2 for 8-year-olds and so
on). Examinations covered only reading, writing and arithmetic and
the code was criticised for having the effect of limiting the range of
education that schools could offer. It is interesting that 5th Standard
was thought to be achievement enough for Alfred rather than
6th Standard, as might have been expected at his age.

2. From this point in the memoir onwards Alfred uses 'Squire' to refer
to his new employer, Benjamin Somers, rather than his father's
former employer, Evan Henry Llewellyn.

3. 'All found' is generally taken to mean 'living in' with all meals
included – the usual arrangement for a pageboy like Alfred. Later
comments in Alfred's memoir suggest, however, that although he
lived at Mendip Lodge at times, he may have more often stayed at
home with his family. The Plumley cottage was situated nearby on
the Mendip Lodge Estate anyway, so this would presumably have
been a satisfactory arrangement for all parties.

4. Stephens, C., *The Reverend Dr Thomas Sedgwick Whalley and the Queen
of Bath* (Cardiff: Candy Jar Books, 2014).

5.   *The Times*, 11 March 1845.

6.   'Aaron Harris' is one of only two or three people given a full name
in Alfred's original text. There is no one of that name registered
as living locally in the census returns for the relevant period but
there is an 'Aaron Hare'. Given the similarity of quite an unusual
name and the small size of the community, this is surely the same
man. In 1891, Mr Hare gives his occupation as 'Missionary' and in
1901 as 'Foreman of the Public Works and Local Preacher', both of
which seem to chime nicely with the image of him called up by
Alfred's description.

7.   Most likely a reference to the famously fat Mr Bumble, the beadle
in Charles Dickens's novel *Oliver Twist*. Although published in
1838, *Oliver Twist* remained hugely popular throughout the whole
of the nineteenth century. In the livery of his trade, the coachman
would surely have put people in mind of Mr Bumble in his beadle's
uniform. This Bumble's real name may have been Joseph Gray, the
only coachman at Mendip Lodge in the 1881 census.

8.   Assuming that the head housemaid is the same member of staff who
was in post at the 1881 census as the under housemaid then Alfred
has used a real name here and Annie is Annie Lovell, aged 20 (in
1886) and born locally.

9.   Again assuming no change from the 1881 census then the sled-
building butler-cum-conjurer is Charles Masters, aged 35 in 1886.
Like Annie Lovell, above, Charles was born locally. It is interesting to
note that locally born staff were in a minority at Mendip Lodge at
the 1881 census. The cook and housekeeper were both Scots (from
Aberdeenshire and Perthshire respectively); the upper housemaid
and kitchen maid were both from Brighton; and Edgar Moyes, one
of Sam's predecessors as footman, was from London.

10. The Blue Grotto is a sea cave on the coast of Capri. A quirk of the
way the sunlight passes through holes in the cave wall and through
the seawater causes the water inside the cave to appear a brilliant
blue. By the late nineteenth century, the cave interior had been
painted by numerous European artists, particularly those of the
Romantic movement.

11.   The Prince's Theatre in Park Row in Bristol was particularly famous for its pantomimes. Assuming Alfred's first visit was at Christmas 1886 then the party from Mendip Lodge would have seen a performance of *Sinbad the Sailor*. www.its-behind-you.com.

12.   The USS *Enterprise*, the fifth US naval vessel to bear that name was a fully armed, steam and sail driven sloop. Between 1888 and 1889 she made a two-year 'Showing the Flag' tour of European and North African ports, including visits to several British ports. Van Beverhoudt Jr, A.E., *These are the Voyages* (US Virgin Islands: Self-published, 2011).

13.   Presumably, the 'Junction' from which Alfred and Sam are compelled to walk is the station at Yatton, at that time a stop on the main line from Bristol to Exeter. The branch line along which they missed the connection would have been the Cheddar Valley Line from Yatton to Wells. The stop that they had planned to get to was most likely the second stop on the Cheddar Valley Line, Sandford & Banwell, 4 miles from Burrington. The 10-mile walk from Yatton back to Mendip Lodge must have been quite an ordeal for Alfred and Sam, especially once they had split up. Neither of them knew the way and there would have been no light at all apart, perhaps, from the moon, if they were lucky. Alfred would only have been 13, Sam may well have been not much older.

14.   A 'four-in-hand' is a carriage or coach pulled by a team of four horses and operated by a single driver. It was the grandest form of private carriage of the period and required a high level of skill from the driver. Prior to the invention of reins that enabled all four horses to be controlled by one driver, four horses required two drivers (or one driver and a postillion – see note 15, below). Alfred's phraseology here suggests that Benjamin Somers may have driven his four-in-hand himself. If so, he was perhaps something of a 'sportsman', for most gentlemen would not have had the requisite skill. Interestingly, Benjamin's father, Thomas Somers, is recorded as having also driven his own carriages, so perhaps Benjamin learned from him. Langford History Group, *More Stories from Langford* (Langford: Langford History Group, 2009).

15. It is implied here, I think, that Squire was now using a pair of horses on his personal carriage rather than a team of four. A 'postillion' was an alternative to a driver or coachman as a means of controlling a pair of horses. Rather than sitting aboard the carriage on a driving seat, the postillion would ride the left-hand horse and control both horses from that position. Although Alfred does not say so, it is perhaps to be understood that Squire desired a postillion purely for reasons of ornament and status while continuing actually to drive the horses himself, otherwise he would have been entrusting his travelling safety to a 12-year-old boy, which seems most unlikely!

16. Rose Stewart, sister of Benjamin Somers – see notes on p. 68.

17. The human Sir Richard Paget was Conservative MP for the neighbouring constituency of Mid-Somerset from 1868 to 1885 and for the nearby city of Wells from 1885 to 1895. One wonders whether the dog – in Alfred's words, 'a most aggressive terrier' – was named in tribute or in jest.

18. This gift is undoubtedly to help support Edward Plumley after he wins his scholarship to teacher-training college (see note 21 to chapter 2). This was no mean gesture – £10 in 1886 was equivalent to around £4,500 in 2016, relative to changes in average earnings (www.measuringworth.com – see note 1 to Family and Circumstances, 1879).

19. Despite the fact that she has not been mentioned before in Alfred's memoir, I think 'my mistress' here must be Agnes Somers, wife of Benjamin Somers. Although Benjamin's mother, Elizabeth, also lived at Mendip Lodge, Agnes would have been mistress of the household. We will never know why Agnes decided Alfred should 'better himself' by taking up an apprenticeship. We can safely assume, though, that she would not have offered to help him in this way if he had not proven himself to be a good, reliable employee who was liked by the Somers family, not least because Agnes also pays Alfred's 'premium' (a one-off fee sometimes required to secure an apprenticeship). It seems unlikely that Alfred's parents would ever have been able to pay an apprenticeship premium for him themselves, particularly since – as Alfred points out a couple of paragraphs later – they were already

helping to fund Edward through college. Agnes's intervention made a huge difference to Alfred's future prospects. It was a life-changing moment for a 15-year-old boy.

20. This was presumably the occasion of the visit to Bristol Docks with Sam the footman.

21. As we have already seen, 'our Member of Parliament' in 1890 was none other than Alfred's father's former employer and Agnes Somers's brother-in-law, Evan Llewellyn. It seems slightly odd that Alfred should refer to Evan in this impersonal way when he had figured so prominently in the earlier section of the memoir. Possibly Alfred was simply trying to avoid the complication of referring to Evan as 'Squire' in a section of the memoir where the term was already being used to refer to someone else.

Family and Circumstances, 1890

1. Roden A., *Great Western Railway: A History* (London: Aurum, 2010).

3. Alfred Plumley: GWR Apprentice

1. 19 June 1890. We know this is the exact date because Alfred gives the date of his reference, collected on the previous day. The date of the reference is the only precise date given by Alfred in the entire memoir.

2. I have read and re-read this paragraph with its curious and excruciating conversation about wind direction and still have no real idea what the doctor was driving at. It is possible that this was just a simple eyesight test but, if so, why was the answer 'Northerly' not sufficient? That answer demonstrated that Alfred could see the weather vane clearly. The conversation obviously unsettled Alfred since it stuck in his mind for over sixty years, but it is not possible to tell from his reporting of it whether he himself understood it or not. Was 'Which way is the wind?' a Victorian euphemism and, if so, for what?

3. Worle Junction, where the Weston Loop left the main line from Bristol.

4. Colza oil is produced from rapeseed and was widely used for all types of oil lamp in the nineteenth century.

5. These milk cans may have been destined for Puxton, the next station, just a couple of miles along on the up-line to Bristol. At Puxton, the London Co-operative Society had built a large creamery with its own railway siding for receiving and processing milk from the dairy farms of south-west England for sale in the capital.

6. Alfred does not explain why tickets for Weston-super-Mare were collected at Worle rather than at Weston itself. Since the passengers would not be leaving the train until it reached Weston, the train presumably remained stationary at Worle until the ticket collectors had walked the full length of it.

7. The pressing need of railway companies to send messages about train movements from one location to another was the most important impetus behind the development of telegraphic communication. In 1839, the GWR became the first railway company to use the system. Messages sent along telegraph wires arrived letter-by-letter. By the time Alfred joined the GWR in 1890 the 'single needle' system had become the national standard. This system generally used Morse code. The receiving instrument in the signal box could be read visually by looking at a needle on a dial where there was a different sequence of movements to the left and /or right for each letter of the alphabet, or it could be 'read' by ear by listening to the two different notes emitted by the machine to correspond with the deflections of the needle. The constant challenge for the receiving operator was to read the instrument quickly enough to write down the message. So simple and practical was the telegraph that it continued in use on many sections of the national railway until well after the Second World War.

8. Alfred's – or rather his landlord's and landlady's – next-door neighbours during the period that Alfred lived in Worle were the Sperring family. George Sperring was killed in an accident at

Weston-super-Mare Station on 31 July 1895, aged 19. The *Wells Journal* reported that he:

> was seen leaning his chest on the buffer of the carriages, with his back turned to the other part of the train, which was shunted close up. Witness on seeing the approaching carriages shouted, 'For God's sake get out of the way!' Deceased, however, seemed paralysed for the moment at the danger that he was in, and before he could leap away he was caught between the two sets of buffers and crushed.

Alfred gives the impression that George's fatal accident occurred during the period covered by the memoir while he (Alfred) was still working at Worle Station. In fact, according to GWR records, by 1895 Alfred was working as a porter at Pill Station on the branch line to Portishead some distance away. Presumably, Alfred had remained in contact with his former colleagues and friends in Worle who told him about George's death and the effect on the Sperring family.

9. Nobbs, P., *The Story of the British and Their Weather: Cloudy with a Chance of Rain* (Stroud: Amberley Books, 2015).

10. Met Office data.

11. Carter, C., *The Blizzard of '91* (Newton Abbot: David & Charles, 1971).

12. Nobbs, P., *The Story of the British and Their Weather*.

13. Carter, C., *The Blizzard of '91*.

14. Eden, P., *Great British Weather Disasters* (London: Bloomsbury, 2009).

15. Simons, P., *Since Records Began* (London: Collins, 2008).

16. Carter, C., *The Blizzard of '91*.

17. 'Rhine' or 'rhyne' is a word local to Somerset and Gloucestershire. It refers to the wide drainage ditches, sometimes fitted with sluice gates and pumps to control the water level, that are used to convert the boggy ground of the Somerset Levels to land suitable for farming.

18. We can help Alfred out here. As we have already seen, the severe frost came two months before the great snowstorm.

19. This method of catching eels remains a living tradition, albeit under a slightly modified name. In his 2012 book, *Wild Hares and Hummingbirds: The Natural History of an English Village* (London: Vintage, 2012), Stephen Moss describes a recent year of living with nature in and around the village of Mark in the Somerset Levels – a village not 20 miles from Alfred's birthplace. One evening the author is taken 'ray-balling' for eels in the River Brue by a group of local people, one of whom learned the practice from his grandfather in the 1950s.

20. This would have been 'Smeaton's Tower' rather than the Eddystone lighthouse itself. Smeaton's Tower stood as a lighthouse at the Eddystone Rocks off Plymouth from 1757 until 1879 when the present lighthouse was built to replace it. The upper part of Smeaton's Tower was dismantled and rebuilt on Plymouth Hoe, opening as a tourist attraction in 1884. It still stands on the Hoe today.

21. Website of the Working Class Movement Library, www.wcml.org.uk.

22. Bronstein, J.L., *Caught in the Machinery: Workplace Accidents and Injured Workers in Nineteenth-Century Britain* (Stanford, California: Stanford University Press, 2008).

23. See the brief history of the NUR published online by the Modern Records Centre at the Library of the University of Warwick (the Modern Records Centre holds the archive of the NUR), www2.warwick.ac.uk/services/library/mrc/.

24. Alfred does not say which union he joined but the likely date (1891) suggests it was perhaps the General Railway Workers' Union, which was founded in 1889.

25. As we will shortly see, Alfred's first move from Worle to Bristol Temple Meads, which he has already mentioned, was most unwelcome to him. His later GWR employment record shows that during his first four years post-apprenticeship he worked as a porter at two stations – first at Nailsea Station and then at Pill Station – followed by a short posting as a signalman to Clifton Bridge in Bristol. After Clifton Bridge he held what was presumably a more settled posting as a signalman at Chippenham in Wiltshire where he stayed for over three years.

26. 'Twenty seven years' is an oddly specific period of time to mention, especially when we know that Alfred worked for the GWR for forty-five years. The implication perhaps is that something caused Alfred to become disillusioned with the trade union movement in or around 1918.

27. Alfred may be referring to the first ever national railway strike, which took place in 1911, almost twenty years after the end of his memoir. The 1911 railway strike is generally seen within the context of the 'Great Unrest', the four or five years immediately prior to the beginning of the First World War. These years saw a number of bitter industrial disputes as workers began to mobilise against the long hours, dangerous conditions and lack of workers' rights that had characterised industrial employment until that point. The 1911 railway strike is summarised in the TUC's online 'History Timeline' (www.unionhistory.info) as follows:

> There was industrial unrest among railway workers due to high prices, long hours and dissatisfaction with the slow moving conciliation system. An unofficial strike started in Liverpool and spread to other cities … The four rail unions made the strike official on 18 August 1911, by which time an estimated 70,000 workers (including 20,000 railway workers) were on strike and troops were mobilised. After Government mediation, the unions' grievances were brought forward to a Royal Commission called to discuss industrial relations in the railways.

28. 'Making a long nose' is an archaic term for the gesture of placing the thumb to the end of the nose, fanning out the fingers and making a wiggling movement with them. The gesture is often used in fun now but in the nineteenth century would have been understood to indicate contempt or derision. Georges, R.A. and Owen-Jones, M., *Folkloristics: An Introduction* (Bloomington and Indianapolis: Indiana University Press, 1995).

29. The Weston-super-Mare Sanitary Laundry was situated in Station Road, Worle. It opened in 1879 and stayed in business for the

next century or so (www.worlehistorysociety.net). A glance at the occupations listed by Worle residents in the 1891 census returns reveals the laundry was comfortably the largest employer in the village at that time.

30. Alfred pays his good friend the respect of using his real name – the only fully verifiable real name in the original memoir. Will Came was the same age as Alfred. He was born in Henbury, then a village in Gloucestershire, but now a suburb of Bristol. In 1891, when he and Alfred met, Will was living with his aunt and uncle, James and Elizabeth Thyer, at Lower Street in Worle.

31. The 'safety bicycle' was first developed during the 1880s as an alternative to the penny-farthing. Safety cycles had front and rear wheels that were either exactly or nearly the same size as each other and were much smaller than the front wheel on a penny-farthing. This development in wheel size facilitated one of the key innovations of the new machines – they allowed the rider to put his or her feet on the ground when the bike was stationary. Safety bicycles were also generally chain driven, rather than the pedals being directly attached to the front wheel.

32. The history of the names and the classes of GWR broad-gauge locomotives can be confusing but *Swallow* was a Rover-class locomotive, as were most of the other locomotives named by Alfred in this paragraph and the next. Most Rover-class locomotives reused names from the earlier Iron Duke class (indeed, some Rover-class locomotives were Iron Duke-class locomotives that had been rebuilt). Rover class were fast, reliable locomotives used to pull express trains on the most important GWR main-line services.

33. The attitude of the average GWR employee of this period, particularly in relation to the broad-gauge service, has been described as 'unshakeably loyal'. Such an employee had 'a tremendous sense of pride in the job, a superiority complex' and believed that the GWR had 'something extra'. Whitehouse, P. and Thomas, D. St J., *The Great Western Railway* (Newton Abbot: David & Charles, 1984).

34. Flying Dutchman was the name given to the GWR's Paddington to Exeter train from 1849 to 1892 (i.e., Flying Dutchman was

the name of a service, not the name of a locomotive). The Flying Dutchman was pulled by Iron Duke-class locomotives and was for many years the world's fastest passenger train, having first set the record in 1848 with an average speed of 58mph.

35.   *Great Bear*, built by the GWR in 1908 and designed by its chief mechanical engineer, George Jackson Churchward (1857–1933), was the first British steam locomotive to have a 4-6-2 wheel arrangement. Locomotives with this wheel arrangement are generally known as Pacific class. In simple terms, the technical advantages of the Pacific-class design are that the 'adhesion' of the locomotive to the track is stronger and the power output is greater, resulting in locomotives that can travel faster for longer. The *Great Bear* was essentially a one-off experiment by the GWR and some railway historians have suggested it was primarily built for its prestige value – it was the largest locomotive in Britain at the time. It was not generally considered a success, not least because its use was limited to the only section of GWR line robust enough to support its weight, that from Paddington to Bristol. The *Great Bear* was retired in 1924. The GWR never built any further Pacific-class locomotives, although the design was widely used elsewhere during the 1920s and '30s, including for such successful and famous locomotives as the *Flying Scotsman* (Great Northern Railway) and the *Mallard* (London & North Eastern Railway). Whitehouse, P. and Thomas, D. St J., *The Great Western Railway*.

36.   Here, Alfred must be referring to the famous experimental exchange of locomotives in 1925 between the GWR and the London and North Eastern Railway (LNER). For a fortnight, the GWR's Castle-class *Pendennis Castle* operated on the LNER's King's Cross to Doncaster service while the LNER's Pacific-class *Victor Wild* ran between Paddington and Plymouth. Both locomotives had their regular drivers. The GWR locomotive, despite being lighter than the LNER's local locomotives, pulled the same trains while using less coal and delivering faster journey times. The following year, a similar trial (without an exchange locomotive this time) saw the GWR's *Launceston Castle* outperform locomotives of the London,

Midland & Scottish Railway (LMS) between Euston and Carlisle. *Railway Wonders of the World* magazine, part 46 (23 December 1935).

37. See note 31 above for a description of the safety bicycle.

38. Alfred was transferred to Nailsea Station – a station, like Worle, on the Bristol to Exeter line – in July 1892. He was to work there as a porter for the next eighteen months. For a period earlier in the nineteenth century, Nailsea, a large village, had had some heavy industry in the form of coal mines and an important glassworks, but by time Alfred moved there most inhabitants were working once again in agriculture. Nailsea is about 10 miles north of Alfred's birthplace and a similar distance south of Bristol.

INDEX